HOOF 'N MOUTH DISEASE

Biblical Monologues
and
How To Do Them

Edward W. Thorn

*With Foreword by
Dr. Raymond Bailey*

CSS Publishing Company, Inc., Lima, Ohio

HOOF 'N MOUTH DISEASE

Copyright © 1998 by
CSS Publishing Company, Inc.
Lima, Ohio

All rights reserved. No part of this publication may be reproduced in any manner whatsoever without the prior permission of the publisher, except in the case of brief quotations embodied in critical articles and reviews. Inquiries should be addressed to: Permissions, CSS Publishing Company, Inc., P.O. Box 4503, Lima, Ohio 45802-4503.

Scriptures marked (RSV) are from the *Revised Standard Version of the Bible*, copyrighted 1946, 1952 (c), 1971, 1973, by the Division of Christian Education of the National Council of the Churches of Christ in the USA. Used by permission.

Scriptures marked (NIV) are taken from the *Holy Bible, New International Version*. Copyright (c) 1973, 1978, 1984 International Bible Society. Used by permission of Zondervan Bible Publishers. All rights reserved.

Scriptures marked (KJV) are from the *King James Version of the Bible*, in the public domain.

Scriptures marked (REB) are from the *Revised English Bible* (REB) copyright (c) Oxford University Press and Cambridge University Press 1989, a revision of *The New English Bible*. Copyright (c) the Delegates of the Oxford University Press and the Syndics of the Cambridge University Press, 1961, 1970. Reprinted by permission.

Scripture quotations marked (NRSV) are from the *New Revised Standard Version of the Bible*, copyright 1988 by the Division of Christian Education of the National Council of the Churches of Christ in the USA. Used by permission.

"Ragman" from *Ragman And Other Cries Of Faith* by Walter J. Wangerin. Copyright © 1984 by Walter Wangerin, Jr. Reprinted by permission of Harper Collins Publishers, Inc.

Excerpt from *An Experience Named Spirit* reprinted with permission of the publisher. Copyright © 1983 by John Shea. Published by Thomas More, A Division of RCL Resources for Christian Living, 200 E. Bethany Drive, Allen, TX 75002.

From *The Circuit Rider*, May, 1994. Copyright © 1994 by The United Methodist Publishing House. Adapted from "The Storyteller's Companion to the Bible," edited by Michael E. Williams. Copyright © 1991 by Abingdon Press. Reprinted by permission.

Library of Congress Cataloging-in-Publication Data

Thorn, Edward W., 1933-
   Hoof 'n mouth disease : biblical monologues and how to do them /Edward W. Thorn.
     p. cm.
   ISBN 0-7880-1167-7 (pbk.)
   1. Monologue sermons. 2. Biographical preaching. I. Title
BV4307.M6M48 1998   97-26640
251--dc21   CIP

This book is available in the following formats, listed by ISBN:
   0-7880-1167-7   Book
   0-7880-1168-5   IBM 3 1/2
   0-7880-1169-3   MAC
   0-7880-1170-7   Sermon Prep

PRINTED IN U.S.A.

*Dedicated to Eldora,
my partner*

ACKNOWLEDGMENTS

Without the response of people with the gift of encouragement this book might never have been written. First on such a list, certainly, is my son Michael, who graciously used his considerable expertise to take photographs. I could go on to name numerous individuals. It is simpler to say that when I was still teaching at Florida Southern College, members of the Crystal Lake United Methodist Church, especially Pastor Roy Lowe, responded to the two monologues I used there in such a way that when I took on the regular chore of part-time pastor at the Lake Lindsey and New Hope United Methodist Churches, I explored the style of monologue preaching still further. Secondly, the people of the First United Methodist Church of Perry, Florida, where I served during the writing of this book, could not have been more receptive. Most helpful was the church secretary, Diane McGuire, who patiently typed and retyped the manuscript. Florence Huth was kind enough to proofread the galley proof. Finally, as I put the finishing touches on the book I am serving part-time at Springhead United Methodist Church; the congregation has encouraged me further in my writings. May the Lord bless these "encouragers," make His face to shine upon them, and prosper all of them in His way.

TABLE OF CONTENTS

Foreword	9
Introduction: Why Monologues?	11

Section 1   17
Original First-Person Biblical Monologues

Hoof 'n Mouth Disease:	
A Monologue of "Rocky Barjona"	19
Satan Goes to Church	31
Gabriel:	
I Was There	41
Homesick:	
Monologue of an Ancient Hebrew	51
Pentecost Communion Meditation:	65
Monologue of a Saint	
Number One Mother	75
It's Hell, I Say:	
Herod Speaks	87
Poolside Blessing:	
Monologue of a Paralytic	99
I Am Zacchaeus	107
Reuben:	
I'm Not a Sandwich	117
Boaz:	
I Am Blessed!	129
Josiah Speaks:	
An Ancient King Brings Greetings	139

Section II
Standard Format Sermons That Include Monologues As Illustrative Material
147

Jesus Is Alive and Well — 151

The End of Babel — 163

We're All in the Same Boat — 173

Section III
Concluding Remarks: Suggestions For Making Monologues
181

Appendix — 195

Bibliography — 199

FOREWORD

Preaching at its best is the embodiment of the gospel of Jesus Christ. Judeo-Christian religion is a flesh and blood one. From Genesis to Revelation there is an unfolding narrative of God's disclosure of God's self to humanity, the apogee of divine creation. Yahweh is a God who talks to people. The Bible is a collection of stories about God's disclosures to His people, His conversations with men and women, and their responses to the divine revelation. The Bible is dramatic literature dominated by characters, plot, conflict, choices and resolutions. Any sermon without reference to persons, without conflict and a climax is flawed.

The narrative that climaxes the collection and provides the controlling metaphor is the New Testament account of Jesus of Nazareth. It is the story of incarnation, of God's identification with humanity. God became flesh and blood to commune with creation in the most intimate way possible — person to person. Clyde Fant expressed it well when he wrote: "The incarnation ... is the truest theological model for preaching because it was God's ultimate act of communication. Jesus, who was the Christ, most perfectly sent God to us because the eternal WORD took on human flesh in a contemporary situation. Preaching cannot do otherwise." All preaching in one form or another should be incarnational — God speaking through women and men to men and women.

Not all preaching reflects either the dramatic character of scripture or the incarnational nature of revelation. Protestant preaching in particular has often been more proposition focused than person focused. Even today some preaching sounds more like debate than revelation. The biblical narratives that most grip readers are the stories about people. The average Christian is much more likely to refer to the story of Hosea and Gomer, or the women taken in adultery, or the relationship of Sarah and Abraham than to any of the household codes or levitical law. People remember Samson, David, Ruth, Jezebel, Ahab, Peter, Lydia, and the other characters who are easier to understand than the most logical of arguments.

Stories and actions are more easily recalled than propositions or even carefully paralleled points in a sermon. Most people do not hear the name of Simon of Cyrene without a mental image of a dark-skinned man bearing the cross for Christ. Mention of Peter, Paul, or Lydia will evoke a favorite story or scene, not a psychological analysis or theological dissertation. The scene of Pilate washing his hands is more vivid than any words he spoke at the trial. Christians speak of God's plan for the world and the church, and it is the plot, the unfolding biblical drama, that comes to mind. Christians brought up in Sunday School are more likely to remember the lessons of Eve and the serpent, Daniel in the lions' den, the Hebrew children in the furnace, the stilling of the storm, and so forth, than they are moralistic sermons. Principles of morality, kindness, and courage are remembered as demonstrations, not as memorized rules of conduct.

One form of preaching that captures eye, ear, and brain of the congregation is the monologue or first-person sermon. Not every preacher will be equally effective in its use, and some may not be able to subordinate self sufficiently to use the monologue technique at all. For those who can, Edward Thorn has written an excellent manual. He provides counsel as to how to do it and models that provide bridges across the centuries. His sermons blend well the horizons of the Bible and the contemporary culturescape. These sermons reduce the profound to the everyday in such a way as to incarnate scriptural truth. One feature found in his book is a section of sermons incorporating the monologue into a more traditional sermon format. Many preachers wanting to try the monologue will find here a way to get their feet wet without total immersion. A word of assurance to those who worry that some modern preaching may not be biblical enough: as a general rule one will find far more Bible in a monologue sermon than in almost any other kind. The sermons in this book are no exception to that rule. Even pastors who never try a monologue sermon will enjoy reading this book and be enriched by the monologues.

Raymond Bailey, Ph.D.

INTRODUCTION: WHY MONOLOGUES?

The idea of using monologues for sermons is not a new one. Hal Holbrook's monologues that bring the character of Mark Twain alive to the audience stirred the imagination of people who flocked to theaters or watched him on television about two decades ago. Clergy have used monologues for decades. Storytelling itself is older than the Bible. The Bible consists largely of stories that arose out of an oral tradition. And, Jesus Himself was a master storyteller — "All these things spake Jesus in parables, and without parables spake he not unto them" (Matthew 13:34, KJV).

The incarnation itself could be viewed, in a sense, as God's living parable. In that "parable," as in no other way, we confront our Creator. The communion service is an enduring parable, or metaphor, for the Christian church. It is in this ceremony that the abstract is made concrete. I once heard a young Roman Catholic priest at St. Joseph's Church in Lakeland, Florida, speak of the wonder of literally holding the body of Jesus. I don't identify with the doctrine of transubstantiation, but I certainly understand the need for the sensory stimulation that comes with seeing and touching the bread and wine.

Monologues are sensual. Those who want to have an intellectualized and sophisticated religious experience may be put off by them. The question is not will the use of monologues reach all people, but will it have a serious impact. The answer is that it did for thousands of years. The oral tradition gave us the creation stories, the flood stories, the synoptic gospels, each of which provided a different emphasis. The Jewish Midrash — stories about Bible stories — was the primary mode of instruction during the time of Jesus. The fact that the average family spends over seven hours a day watching television is witness to the fact that we haven't lost our fascination with stories. Currently, there is a surge of interest in storytelling. Abingdon even has an entire multi-volume commentary series being produced to assist with monologues and other forms of storytelling called *The Storyteller's Companion*.

Why this surge of interest in stories? Richard Jensen asserts that the television generation kids learned to think in stories. His book *Thinking In Story: Preaching In A Post-Literate Age* (CSS Publishing Co., Inc., Lima, Ohio, 1993) is a call to adapt preaching to those who think in story in the electronic age. Oratory, as taught since the time of Aristotle, has a propositional content. It adapted well to the print culture to communicate ideas (Jensen, p. 37ff), but it may not adapt to a portion of our current audience.

Jensen backs up many of his ideas by referring to Neil Postman, especially his book, *Amusing Ourselves To Death*. Both Postman and Jensen seem to be fascinated by the works of Marshall McLuhan (*The Medium Is The Message* and *The Medium Is The Massage*). McLuhan analyzed the society that was born since the advent of electronic media, especially those born since the widespread use of television. McLuhan postulated four ages of man. First, there was the Oral/Aural Age. This age was pre-literate. People learned orally. In this environment all senses were involved. Everywhere, people had their senses bombarded with the activities, life, and information of the tribe. Whatever one member of the tribe knew, the whole village generally knew. This tribal period was followed by the Alphabetic Age. There was an attempt for a few to put down on stone, papyrus, or other materials history that could be passed on. An elite class developed who, because they could read, had more knowledge. For those elite, the sense of the eye became more important. The third age is the Gutenberg Age. When Gutenberg invented the printing press, he made it possible to copy books at a fairly rapid rate. Books became inexpensive. Eventually literate people became the norm in the west. McLuhan asserts that as a result of literacy, there was a separation of the senses in the acquisition of information. Instead of getting information in a bombardment of senses like a kaleidoscope, as people did in the oral/aural age, the senses were separated. People became sequential in their thought processes, following the sequential, propositional nature of reading material. But now we are in the fourth age — the Electronic Age. People's senses are again bombarded from every corner. Johnny sometimes can't read well. It may be because Johnny doesn't gather information that way.

Johnny also may not follow the propositional, sequential thinking of the traditional sermon.

Many of us aren't comfortable with the changes that have come in the worship styles of many growing churches — the use of synthesizers, bands, guitars, and even dance. The electronic machines bombard the senses. They speak in the "language" of the baby boomers and baby busters. The gospel itself does not change, but some accommodation to this generation's method of gathering information may be essential.

Why use monologues? Why have monologues become important for use in sermons in the nineties? A generation raised on television is used to drama in which there are characters with whom they can identify. Such characters face tensions and conflicts they must resolve. Monologues depict Biblical characters who also confronted similar problems they resolved for good or ill. Monologues delve into the history, the times, the mind of the character, and attempt to draw subtle parallels between their situations and that of contemporary Americans.

In the telling of a story through monologue-style sermons, people relate not only to the character, but also the action format. The format of television is storytelling. Even the news — perhaps especially the news — is a storytelling format. It isn't like the old days of radio news when an announcer read facts. Early television news did the same. John Cameron Swayze, and others of that time, sat before a camera, merely reading facts. The evening news was fifteen minutes long. An occasional still picture of a person or a scene was shown in the background. With the advent of satellite television, news was lengthened — at first to a thirty-minute format — then CNN gave us 24 hours of storytelling. We saw live people at war in Vietnam. People were shot before our eyes. Is that part of the reason people responded to its horrors significantly differently from previous wars? We saw millions starving in Africa before our very eyes. People gave millions of dollars to the cause as long as the cameras were glued to their camps. We literally saw the beginning of the Gulf War with explosives flashing against the background of the night sky. We were hypnotized by the scene of O. J. Simpson in his Bronco being "chased" by the police down

Los Angeles freeways. The sales of Broncos rose significantly immediately after the television broadcasts and rebroadcasts. Storytelling fascinates people. International news daily captures large audiences. It is one of the most consistent revenue producers for both local stations and the networks.

The other television programs are dramas or talk shows in which people share their stories. Dramas and talk shows, like Biblical stories, have characters, conflicts, described or visual scenes, perhaps a moral, and a plot in which people attempt to resolve their conflicts. The monologue does all of the above. It is a format people are used to. They tend to get excited about it, especially those born in the television generation. These people are much less likely to get their sources of information and entertainment from the daily newspaper and other written forms of communication than previous generations.

Another reason people relate to the genre of the monologue is that the use of monologues disarms individuals. The old-style sermon tends to point the finger. It is argumentative. If it uses stories as illustrations, those stories are part of the evidence for the moral argument. They are much more direct in their nature. Monologues are indirect. The person is merely telling his or her story. She, or he, tells about his or her personal conflict situation, how it was resolved, and what was learned from it. The story becomes the point. It may or may not use some directive in encouraging the listener to thought or action in the conclusion. Such directiveness is, at most, nominal. The danger in the traditional sermon is that the direct moralization may result in defensiveness, or sometimes guilt. In the monologue, if the listener identifies with the character, she or he can say, "Aha, that's where I too went wrong," or, "Aha, I wonder if the solution the character followed can assist me." Richard Jensen (*Thinking In Story*, page 62) says, "The telling of Biblical stories and of stories which help us to experience Biblical stories have a chance to get around ... cultural filters. We don't see what is coming in the story. When we do, it is too late. We are hooked by the story." Nathan, the prophet, hooked David with the story of a poor family's pet sheep that was confiscated by a rich man. Only when David passed judgment did Nathan reveal to him that he, David, was that tyrant. To have broached the subject directly might have cost Nathan his head — at the least, his job as "palace prophet."

Finally, the monologue story can, therefore, be healing. "News and Trends" (*Psychology Today,* vol. 25, September 1992, p. 8) reports that Laura Chasin, a family therapist, got an idea for healing from watching television. In her job, she saw how overheated people become as they get polarized by intellectual argumentation. She got the combatants to recast their beliefs as personal stories and experience. Switching the focus from arguments to stories of personal experience highlights similarities more than differences. People discover they are all struggling with the same values, uncertainties and complexities. It helps them to rethink issues in a broader context. In *Circuit Rider* (May, 1994, p. 5), Tim O'Brien is quoted as saying that writing novels about Vietnam assisted him in dealing with unresolved problems. He is not the only one who is helped. One female reader wrote to him to say, "Now I understand why my husband cries at night, or wakes up screaming." The story/monologue does more than clarify. It is participatory. It invites the listener to participate in the reality of the story, i.e., the conflict and its resolution. In watching a drama, the audience is moved sensually. Persons experience emotions, and may even be driven to tears or terror. The objective is to make them more than observers, i.e., to become vicariously a part of the drama.

In *The Seven Day A Week Church*, Lyle Schaller (Abingdon Press, Nashville, p. 61) quotes George Plagenz, a syndicated religion writer, comparing the pulpit with the theater. "Theater is something done with an audience in view. It must, therefore, be stimulating to the ear, the eye and the mind of the members of the audience. If preaching is theater, good preaching is good theater."

In the first section of this book, there are twelve manuscripts of my personally developed monologues. In section two, there are examples of how monologues may be incorporated in traditional sermons. I use only three examples. These are monologues "borrowed" from others. In general, I have difficulty just taking a monologue from someone else and using it. This is one way I have come to terms with this uncomfortable issue. The sermon maker, however, is not limited to integrating other people's monologues into the sermon. One can also write his or her own original monologues that stand alone, or incorporate them into the traditional sermon. The third section attempts briefly to answer some questions with regard to how to create and perform monologues.

SECTION I

**Original First-Person
Biblical Monologues**

HOOF 'N MOUTH DISEASE:
A MONOLOGUE OF "ROCKY" BARJONA
Mark 8:27-35

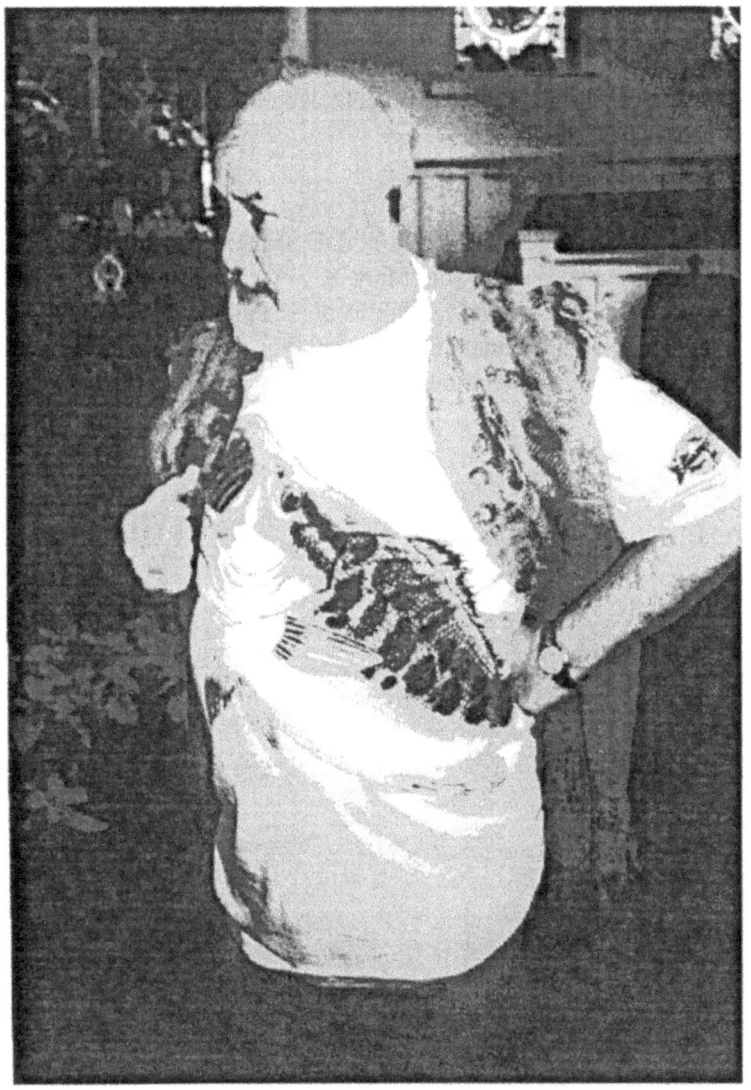

THEME:
Peter is like many of us who preach. He thinks he must talk, even when he has little to say.

SETTING FOR THE MONOLOGUE SERMON:
The lectionary reading was Mark 8. It was the Lenten season. What does it mean for Messiah to die? Peter wrestles with that eventuality in a manner that we Monday morning quarterbacks sometimes can't quite comprehend.

HOOF 'N MOUTH DISEASE:
A MONOLOGUE OF "ROCKY" BARJONA
Mark 8:27-35

In the year 1988, the Democratic Convention opened with a bleached blonde,
> whose time on terra firma was enough to designate her "numerically challenged,"
>> speaking of the then Republican presidential candidate.

Her startling introduction began with the words:
> "Poor George, he cain't help it;
>> he was born with a silver foot in his mouth."

That somewhat abrasive statement brought down the house,
> and it eventually ushered Ann Richards into the Texas governor's mansion.

I cannot say I, Peter, was born with a silver foot in my mouth,
> but there are certainly more than a few who assert
>> that I was born with "hoof and mouth disease."

I guess people are pretty much the same —
> no matter what era,
>> or country they were born in.

Almost two millennia have gone by, but I, Simon Peter —
> (By the way, "Peter" means "rock" —
>> that was what people called me — Rocky) —

Anyway, I, Peter, or Rocky, remember some of my awkward remarks like they were yesterday.

Thank God, with my ruddy complexion,
> it was not too easy to discern that my cheeks were burning.

That ruddiness didn't all come from the imbibing of liquid "refreshment" as might be rumored.

I was a fisherman.

We fishermen work out in the sun and the wind,
> the rain,
>> the snow.
It was a rough life —
> not one in which one practices social niceties —
>> acquires a smooth tongue,
>>> or learns the vocabulary of a diplomat.
Our vocabulary was — uhh —
> somewhat different, too, from church talk,
>> though it certainly was sprinkled with some "theological"
>> verbiage.

I thought my life would go on like this forever.
For centuries the men of my family had been fishermen —
> my father,
>> my grandfather,
>>> my great-grandfather —
When I was born, my father, Jonah, was glad that I was a boy —
> because, he said, "Simon can help me at my trade."
When a second son, Andrew, was born, Father was overjoyed.
In time Andrew and I, along with our good friends James and
John, formed a most effective fishing team.
Even though all of us had our spiritual yearnings,
> I don't think it ever occurred to us that we would be anything
> but fishermen —
>> certainly not rabbis.
We were hardly the rabbi type.

You in twentieth century America can barely understand what it
meant to change one's vocation.
You folks do it all the time.
Back then one usually learned the family trade —
> had a certain niche in life —
>> and we never aspired to anything else.
Indeed, when the Master called us to follow him,
> we left our nets —
>> but we also kept our boats and equipment.

You may have noticed in your gospels that we were in our boats
quite a lot —
    we continued to be fishermen at times.
It never dawned on us that we might become rabbis.
Jesus even preached from my boat once when the mob kept
pushing closer and closer along the Galilean Sea.
And —
    do you not recall —
        even after the resurrection —
            Jesus came to see us on several occasions.
Yet, we all went back to fishing.
It was a familiar outlet.
It was something we understood.
It was only as we met with Him on the beach one post-
resurrection day while we were fishing —
    and He fried fish for us,
        He did —
            He sat down and had breakfast with us on the beach —
            that I fully responded to my call.

I confess that each time He came to us, I had mixed emotions.
I loved Him, but I had failed Him —
    I who had boldly proclaimed that though everyone else might
    desert Him —
        He could depend on me!
That very night, however, I denied that I ever knew Him.

On the beach —
    He met us where we were —
        not where we ought to be —
            but where we were —
                as we ate the fish —
                      three times He asked, "Peter, do you love me?"
I was in anguish as I replied, "Lord, you know I love you."
Each time I replied, He commanded, "Feed my sheep."
That, for me, was a moment of truth —
    about my vocation —
        and about my glib speech.

Often I ran off at the face before I got my brain in gear.
I've since discovered that when the mind goes blank
it is wise to switch off the mouth.
I meant well, but I was a much better talker than I was a listener.
So many times —
    example: the woman who had an issue of blood for twelve
    years — to herself she kept saying,
    "If I could but touch the hem of his garment,
        I would be healed."
When she slipped in among the crowd and touched Jesus,
    He stopped and said loudly, "Someone touched me!"

"Of course — of course, Master," I said impatiently —
    "the crowd is so close, they're touching all of us!"
I didn't wait for Him to clarify what He meant,
    I just shot off my motormouth.

Jesus ignored me and said again, "Someone has touched me —
    power has gone out from me."
The woman came forward, knelt before him, proclaiming that she
was the one,
    and that she was healed.

We followed Jesus, the twelve of us —
    followed Him for three years.
We ministered with Him, and for Him.
We were glad to be "insiders" with the Messiah.
We were expecting to have positions of power in His soon
coming kingdom.
Then He threw us a curve ball — anachronistically speaking.
Jesus had just miraculously fed four thousand people.
We were certain He was the Messiah.
Afterwards we walked on to other villages to minister.
Along the way Jesus asked us,
    "Who do people say I am?"

We replied,
   "Well, some say 'John the Baptist,'
     others 'Elijah,'
        and some 'one of the prophets.' "
But Jesus pressed us further with another question.
   "Who do you say that I am?"
Like always, I was the one that answered the question.
The others took time to measure their answers to these questions very deliberately.
Not me!
I just responded, "You are the Messiah" —
   to which Jesus said, "Blessed are you Rocky, Son of Jonah."
Then He began to teach us —
   and here's where the curveball came —
     teach us that He would suffer many things;
       be rejected of the chief priests, the elders
         and the teachers of the law —
           resulting in His death —
              but that in three days He would rise again.
Well, I hardly hesitated!
I took him aside and began to rebuke Him —
   "No way, Lord" —
     "Not you" —
       I didn't want to hear it.
I guess what I was trying to say to Jesus was that death could permanently hurt Him —
   for a long time.

Or let me state it in an even more modern and politically correct way —
   "Jesus," I said, "death could be very injurious to your wellness potential."
I just had His best interest in mind —
   and of course my interests, too.

Turning to the disciples, however, Jesus began to rebuke me.
He got right up into my face and said,
"Get behind me, Satan.

You do not have in mind the things of God,
    but the things of men."
Talk about getting one's foot in one's mouth;
I turned crimson.
I was confused.
How could this happen?
How could He suffer death at the hands of mere mortals?
He had the power to prevent it.
What about us?
We had invested three years in this venture.
Our fishing business had suffered.
Now, He was saying it was all for naught —
    at least that's what we heard.

Six days later He took me, James, and John with Him up a high mountain.
There He was transformed before our very eyes.
His face shone like the sun.
Even His clothes were transformed into a dazzling whiteness that no bleach in the world could create.
Then I understood what the scriptures were saying when they reported that after Moses had seen the back of God on Mount Sinai, upon receiving the ten commandments —
    his face shone so brightly
        that no person could look on it.
In fact, Moses and Elijah met with Jesus on this mountain
and conversed with him as we watched.

And of course —
    frightened and not knowing what to say,
        but never at a loss for words,
           I blurted out, "Lord,
              Lord,
                  it's good for us to be here.
                      Let us put up three shelters:
                          one for you,
                              one for Moses, and
                                  one for Elijah."

Then a cloud appeared and enveloped them,
> and a voice came from the cloud:
>> "This is my beloved Son; listen to Him."

Suddenly we looked around and no one was there but Jesus.
As we went down the mountain, Jesus commanded us to tell no one about this until He was raised from the dead.
For once I was at a loss for words —
> but not for questions.

James, John, and I kept discussing among ourselves what Jesus meant about "rising from the dead,"
> but we said nothing to the others.

I'm sure you are wondering how I could have been so stupid —
> how I could hear Him say again and again that He would die and rise again,
>> but fail to believe, to comprehend it —
>>> to even experience it and still not comprehend.

It's a matter of focus —
> selective perception.

Let me explain it this way.
While I speak to you, some of you are daydreaming —
> about an upcoming vacation,
>> about a meeting with a friend or family member,
>>> or even your boss.

Others of you are carrying burdens —
> grief,
>> physical discomfort,
>>> disappointment,
>>>> or anxiety.

Still others will at times whisper to a friend
> and miss part of what I say —

Indeed, everyone of you has, at points in my narrative,
> been distracted —
>> even though almost all of you are tuning in to me at some points,
>>> everyone of you has daydreamed
>>>> as I have been speaking.

As a consequence,
> each of you is hearing a slightly different message.

That's selective perception.

There is also a matter of expectation, and belief systems, through which we filter all information.
Indeed, we avoid information that is contrary to strongly held beliefs.
We expected a Messiah that was very politically powerful —
> a world ruler over the kingdoms of this world.

We thought Jesus would do this, and do it now.
We simply tuned out any hint of vulnerability.

Let me illustrate from an event in your time.
In the early '60s it was discovered that there was a clear connection between health and the use of tobacco.
The American Cancer Society wrote up the information in pamphlet form —
> put such pamphlets in public places for people to read.

Guess who read them —
> not the smokers who needed the information,
>> but the non-smokers,
>>> three to one.

We tend to seek information that confirms our deeply held beliefs and ignore those sources of information that don't support our beliefs,
> because such information is uncomfortable to deal with.

That's known as "selective exposure."

Furthermore, if we are exposed to information contrary to our strongly held beliefs,
> we tend to be much more likely to forget it,
>> than do those who find the information confirming their beliefs.

That's called "selective retention."
Between selective perception,
> selective exposure, and

      selective retention,
           it is difficult to change a person's basic belief system.
Something like that was happening with me and all of us.
He spoke of suffering, death, and servanthood.
We dreamed of royalty, palaces, and power.
We simply weren't listening —
Instead of contemplation, I was engaged in insensitive and
excessive articulation —

But, somehow, Jesus knew me better than I knew myself —
    He chose me —
        and I am a privileged man!
He has taken this voice of mine that has gotten me in so much
trouble —
    and used it to help others find themselves —
        three thousand people responded to my message of the
            kingdom on the day of Pentecost alone.
Over and over He, the Savior, has used this voice.

At least I don't suffer from stage fright —
My friend, the apostle Paul,
    who wrestled much with God over his frailties,
        reports that he had the distinct impression
            that the Almighty was saying to him,
                "My grace is sufficient for you, Paul."
But additionally, He said something we often don't hear.
He said, "My strength is made perfect in your weakness."
I don't know what his problem was —
    something about "thorns" —
        but in his very weakness God used him.

I guess that's my message to you:
What others,
    indeed you yourself,
        consider to be your greatest fault, may,
            from a divine viewpoint,
                be your greatest asset —

when that troublesome characteristic is
consecrated to Him.
If the Lord can take an unpolished, raw fisherman like me,
He can use you too.
"Hoof and mouth disease" —
you better believe it —
no question I got it —
but what is more important is that the Lord has me —
all of me,
including my mouth.

SATAN GOES TO CHURCH
Job 1:1; 2:1-10

THEME:
Satan is not a gruesome Halloween figure. Rather, he is remarkably attractive, very much like us, and frequently not only fools, but also uses us for his own devious purpose.

SETTING FOR THE SERMON MONOLOGUE:
The lectionary called for a sermon on Job. The book of Job invites us to explore the problem of evil. People are fascinated by evil. Why not? It's in them. It's in their environment. Some watch horror shows about him. He seems like a Halloween figure. The Biblical Satan is not always so sinister in appearance. Indeed, he can be quite attractive when he wishes to be. To understand Satan is in a measure to understand ourselves. This may not be — almost certainly is not — my best sermon — but it has provoked more talk than any other.

SATAN GOES TO CHURCH
Job 1:1; 2:1-10

Surprised to see me in church?
There are a lot of myths about me.
I'm here to tell my side of the story.
I come here, or send one of my emissaries here quite often.
All of you have a certain kinship with me.
Some of you are rather fussy about it.
You try to resist me,
    but I know your weaknesses.
Sooner or later I get to you.
Others of you rather enjoy your "deviltry,"
    giggle about it and go on.
Actually, "you all" —
    ohh,
        surprised at the "y'all"?
I come from the south too, you know —
    deep —
        deep south, according to legend.
Anyway, you who enjoy your deviltry can laugh a little at your humanity
    and just expect the grace of Yaweh to sustain you.
I don't refer to the outright "sinners" who revel in their sinfulness.
I don't even have to control them.
They're like a snowball going downhill.

Some of you look at me rather strangely when I mention snowballs.
You've got an expression about the "chance of a snowball in hell."
I know about snowballs.
I get around —
    up north,
        down south,

North America,
    Asia,
        Africa.
I'm no stranger to any place —
    or for that matter, any time.
I'm well acquainted with your grandfathers and grandmothers,
    and all your ancestors going clear back to the time of Adam —
        and before —
            but I'm getting ahead of my story.
I was talking about those of you who make good servants —
    ambassadors for me,
        and those who don't.
You probably imagine that those snowball types are my best representatives.
In many respects they are,
    but not all of them.
It's helpful to have the ne'er-do-well,
    the fallen down drunken bum,
        the rapist
            and the serial murderer on my side.
Actually they're not my best advertisement, however.
Very few people want to be like them —
    though you'd be surprised how many are titillated by movies about Bonnie and Clyde,
        or Thelma and Louise,
            when it is "artfully" presented.
I can usually count on big money in my bank when such movies come out.
All kinds of impressionable young people are influenced by such stories,
    when one of my helpers thoroughly presents the glamorous side of it.
Actually, we're quite truthful, you know.
We do present the downside to it too,
    but that's not the emphasis.
For some, there's always the thrill that they,
    in their imaginations,
        "might could" beat the odds.

Some of those, who actually follow through and imitate,
> don't even care that they might get caught.

The "thrill" of it all makes it worthwhile to them.

In all our advertising messages, we emphasize "thrill";
> that seems to work quite well.

Between "thrill" and "comfort,"
> we finally get all of you to assist us in our endeavors —
> > our "work."

Sometimes the most "spiritual,"
> the super-religious,
> > the super-pious
> > > are the most helpful of all to our cause.

They work hard for your God.
They try so hard to be good —
> to refrain from sin.

Sometimes I even lay off these "do-gooders" for a while.
Let them become "respectable,"
> admired by hordes of other "do-gooders" as heroes of the
> faith.

But, the bigger they are,
> the harder they fall.

When they do fall,
> then it discourages many other "do-gooders."

You'd be amazed how many people I've made desert the faith,
> after a fall by a famous evangelist.

Aren't we devils!?!

When these people get real good, often they think they're special —
> unlike the rest of you mortals.

Even if I can't get some of these people to openly disgrace
themselves,
> I can still use them.

They're some of my best servants.
They're the worst advertisement for God there is.
They're grumpy;
> they gossip;
> > they criticize.

They don't even need to say much aloud.
In time they develop beady little eyes, above a beak-like nose,
    a face that has an almost perpetual expression of disapproval.
Whenever someone is thinking about giving his or her life to
    Christ, or serving my enemy in wholesome ways,
        I just have them encounter the "super-spiritual" and ask,
           "Do you want to be like them?"
When Job was ill, I sent three men of that ilk to minister to him.
Their "ministrations" were enough to send Job into real spasms.

Others,
    like your pastor,
        are creampuffs.
He's always thinking,
    "I've gotta lose weight.
        I gotta lose weight.
           Gotta quit eating so much.
                Gotta quit eating so much."
He keeps worrying about those delicious delicacies that he
promises Jesus he'll give up.
All I have to do is keep planting in his mind the thought
    "don't think about food —
        don't think about food" —
           that image of a dish of candied ice cream sends him
                straight to the refrigerator.
He loves the thrill of food.
Most people have some kind of obsession,
    attitude,
        habit,
           or addiction that they try hard to avoid —
                but we put the pressure on them —
                      frequently by making them think of what they're
                          not going to do.
As long as the idea is repetitiously in their head,
    we've got our foot in the door —
Pressure builds up like a pressure cooker with no outlet valve.
Sooner or later we get them!

Sometimes your pastor tries to balance that diet problem with exercise,
> but he loves to be comfortable.

In July, he bought an expensive treadmill —
> he got serious.

He spent almost a thousand dollars for it —
> Sears' best.

He used it regularly,
> but as he got up speed the machine would go berserk under his weight.

By the time the repairman got out to look,
> and tell him the machine wouldn't work at an appropriate speed with his paunch,
>> and he returned it to the store, three weeks went by —
>>> no exercise.

Then he bought a good exercise bike.
It broke before he made one complete turn of the pedal —
Sears sent out a repairman who determined that the entire frame would have to be replaced.
By the time all that gets done,
> Ed will have an excuse not to exercise over a period of six comfortable,
>> no-sweat weeks.

He has a thirteen-hundred dollar Nordic Flex™ World Class Gym that he's only used two or three times,
> because it's "too complicated."

We're working towards giving him another heart attack —
> one to make him retire,
>> and he plays right into our hands.

Aren't we devils!?!

Some of God's people are more stalwart.
My "friend" Job was one.
Now there was a challenge.
I got in the face of the Creator,
> and said that there was only one reason Job served him so well —

        because he was handsomely rewarded for it —
          wealth,
            health,
              and a beautiful family.
God let me test him.
I took away his wealth;
    Job responded, "The Lord gives and the Lord takes away —
    blessed be the name of the Lord!"
I annihilated his family —
    his response,
        "The Lord gives and the Lord takes away;
        blessed be the name of the Lord."
I gave him dreadful diseases.
His own wife said, "Job, curse God and die!"
His first response —
    "Shall we accept good from God and not trouble?"

Because of these kinds of responses,
    you folks often speak of the "patience of Job."
It took him longer than most,
    but as time went on he was anything but patient —
        particularly after I sent those hyperspiritual critics
        to instruct and "comfort" him.
They wore him down.
In time he was shaking his fist in the very face of God,
    but I must say he retained his faith.
Eventually, the Heavenly One made his point with me.
You can't win them all —
    but I certainly do win my share.

I understand that you're going to have communion now.
Communion services make me slightly ill —
    all that stuff about "sacrifice"
        and "atonement."
It's time for me to leave.
By the way, if you don't think I have some influence in this church,

just note how regularly many of your fellow worshipers
   don't show up on Communion Sunday —
      think about it.

You've not noticed me here before because of some of the myths about me.
Some of you actually think I come with horns and forked tail.
Remember that I was created to be one of the most beautiful,
   intelligent,
      and powerful of all the angels.
When I come,
   I come in many forms,
      but almost always, I come as an attractive being —
         even as an angel of light.
I visited you many times —
   you just didn't recognize me because you expected an evil-looking person.
I'll visit you again —
   some other time,
      some other form —
         But, I'll most certainly be seeing you.

As they say, "See you in church!"

GABRIEL: I WAS THERE
Luke 1:13-19, 26-35

THEME:
Salvation history is not a series of whimsical happenings. What happens is by design. The Biblical witness suggests not only a loving God, but cosmic evil forces in combat with the Almighty. The archangel Gabriel shares all this from the perspective of an "eyewitness."

SETTING FOR THE SERMON MONOLOGUE:
I have used this monologue on two occasions. The first time, I used it in slightly different form for Easter. The second time, I wrote it for Christmas. With slight modification, it could be used for any Sunday.

GABRIEL: I WAS THERE
Luke 1:13-19, 26-35

You look out into the sky and call it the heavens.
You look beyond that immediate atmosphere you see into space,
    where your mighty spaceships have explored.
You see the sun, the moon and the stars.
That, too, you call heaven.
But I come from a place, beyond time and space,
    that you also call heaven.
I am Gabriel.
The gospel of Luke tells you of my words to Zechariah
announcing to the old man and his barren wife
    the conception of a son, John the Baptist.
"I stand in the presence of God, and I bring good news," I said.

Because of my unique position —
    standing in the presence of God,
        I have been privy to the plans of the councils of heaven.
I have listened to the dreams of the Almighty;
    I have also seen the attempts to thwart those dreams
        and purposes.
Let me assure you that He is the Almighty —
    the King of Kings —
        Lord of Lords —
            there is none like Him.
It may seem, though, at times, that His plans are being derailed —
    that evil and injustice are triumphing.
The message of the birth of a babe in Bethlehem —
    the message of the empty tomb is that He,
        the Creator has won —
He — the Creator — shall continue to win —
    and that the kingdoms of this world
        shall become the kingdoms of our Lord —
            and of His Christ.
Yes, I was there.

I was there when Lucifer, the beautiful one,
   the shining one,
      rebelled and led one third of the angelic beings in an
      attempt to dethrone God.
Lucifer lost the battle, but still war rages on in the heavens.
The plans and schemes made there are often carried out on the earth.

But —
   the Lord God, the Creator continued His creative work.
He created the earth, the sun, the moon and the stars.
I saw the Lord breathe the breath of life into man —
   and man, Adam, became a living being,
      made in the likeness of his Creator.
And God looked upon His entire creation —
   and "behold it was good."

It did not remain so, however.
The evil schemes of the Shining One —
   Lucifer,
      the Satan,
         perverted the purpose of God in His creation.
A terrible darkness settled over the earth.
It looked as though the Satan had won.
Sin, disease, injustice became rampant in the world.
Men slaughtered one another.
The self-centered ego of man became ascendant —
   you would have thought the Satan was their father.
Certainly, mankind followed him and his ways.

But, God dreamed another dream.
His children were gone astray,
   but He would single out a people,
      the descendants of Abraham and Sarah,
         to represent Him and point the way back to Himself.
However, Sarah was infertile;
   again, it appeared that Lucifer had won.

But —
> in her old age God created life in her womb —
>> with, of course, a little assistance from Abraham.

A people was launched to represent Him.

The Lord had hardly won that battle,
> when the Satan launched a new offensive.

The great destroyer launched a famine in the land of Abraham's descendants that threatened to destroy them.

My God is a winner, however,
> and He made provision for His people.

The grandson of Abraham —
> the Sons of Israel,
>> went into Egypt —
>>> won favor for them with the Pharaoh.

Lucifer was undaunted.

In time, he made the Israelis seem to be a threat to the Egyptians.

To wipe out the future of the race,
> he induced the new Pharaoh to decree
>> that all male descendants of Abraham be killed
>>> as soon as they were born.

But I, who stand in the presence of God,
> saw the Almighty counter
>> by warming the heart of Pharaoh's own daughter towards one tiny Israelite male —
>>> Moses —

It was this Moses who led His people out of Egypt —
> out of slavery.

In fact he became the great lawgiver —
> the one who transmitted the very laws of God to the people.

We angels looked on the ingenuity and majesty of God with wonder and delight.

But —
> the Israelites did not always honor their Creator and His laws in their hearts.

They often forsook Him and followed after false gods —
    gods inspired by the Satan himself —
        whose ways "led the people into destruction."
They became weak and captive to other nations.

Still the Almighty was working out a plan —
    He would send His only son to make a way,
        and show that way to this mass of confused humanity.
He would be born of a virgin as a special sign.
He would be the second Adam.
In the first Adam men would all die.
In the second Adam, all would be made alive.
I myself, Gabriel, brought the message to Mary that she would be the mother of this child —
    the child whose birth you celebrate this day.

Satan does not give up easily, however.
He had a decree go out from the ruler Herod that all male Israeli babies in the Bethlehem area be put to death.
But, my God, in whose presence I stand,
    whispered into the ear of Joseph,
        Mary's husband to be,
            to flee into Egypt, taking Mary and the lad along.
When Herod was dead, Joseph, Mary, and Yeshua returned to Israel, and settled in Nazareth.
I watched him grow up.
He was "some kind" of a boy.
He became "some kind" of a man.
At age thirty, He became a rabbi,
    and kept saying He was uniquely related to the Father —
        that to see Him was to see the Father.
He indeed embodied the essence of the Father,
He also reflected humanity's own highest aspirations.
The people loved him —
    perhaps too much.
It aroused jealousy in religious leaders.

The Satan used the jealousy, as well as the pettiness of the
Roman leaders and some of the Jewish rabbis and priests
    to have Him executed.
So much for the plans of the Creator.
It appeared to be all over.
His execution was awesome and bloody.
It was a terribly dark moment.
The skies rumbled —
    literal darkness swept the land —
        an earthquake ravished Jerusalem.
Even Yeshua, hanging on a cross, was heard to say,
        "My God! My God!
            Why have you forsaken me!"

Moments later, as the earth and skies split apart,
    the "Savior" of mankind was heard to yell,
        "It is finished!"

It seemed hopeless.
All was silent.
The curtain that limited access to the Holy of Holies in the
temple,
    the temple where He had so often taught,
        was split from bottom to top!

In hell, Lucifer and his demonic angels were heard to be uttering
loud,
    raucous,
        sardonic laughter.

Please forgive this anachronistic depiction,
    but can you imagine the Saturday morning obituary in the
    Jerusalem Post, if this had happened in your time?
It would read:
    Yeshuah Bar Joseph, age 33, citizen of Nazareth.
    He was a carpenter until three years ago
        when he became a self-appointed,
            itinerant
                rabbinical teacher.

Loved by many, he was nonetheless controversial.
He was rejected in his own city of Nazareth.
Members of his own synagogue once attempted to stone him
for blasphemy:
He had made himself equal to Yaweh.
Several of his own brothers proclaimed him mad.

Still others called him Lord,
    the Messiah,
        the deliverer,
            King of the Jews —
                the one who would throw off the yoke of the
                Romans.
He was executed yesterday as a revolutionary.
He died on a criminal's cross during the time of the
earthquake.
He was buried in the tomb of one Joseph of Arimathea.
He leaves behind his mother Mary,
    an unknown number of brothers and sisters,
        numerous friends and followers.
No memorial service has been announced.

Early Sunday morning,
    they would have interrupted the regularly scheduled
        program on Jerusalem TV networks with the following
            news announcement:
"Officials are alarmed at the discovery that the body of
    Yeshua Bar Joseph,
        the revolutionary who was crucified on Friday,
            is missing.
He called himself the Son of God,
    and declared that if executed,
        He would rise again on the third day.
Guards were posted at His tomb to insure that His body could
not have been snatched.
Even though it is a capital offense to do so,
    the guards have stated they fell asleep.

When they awoke, the tomb was empty.
JTV looked for the guards to confirm or deny the rumor.
The guards are being held in seclusion,
    and may not be interviewed.
Reporters on the scene at the mouth of the tomb confirm that
the very large stone covering the opening
    has been rolled away.
The tomb itself is empty.
We'll update as we receive more news —
    now back to our regularly scheduled program."

I, Gabriel, was there at the empty tomb.
I observed as my fellow angels joyfully announced to the two
weeping Marys and Joanna that He is alive —
    alive forevermore.

And in heaven, I, Gabriel, who stand in the presence of God,
    saw the elders and the angels —
        ten thousands by ten thousands,
            gathered around the throne,
                prostrate before the ascended Son.
In a loud voice they were singing,
    "Worthy is the Lamb, who was slain,
    to receive power and wealth
        and wisdom and strength
            and honor and glory and praise!

    To Him who sits on the throne and to the Lamb be praise and
    honor and glory and power
        for ever and ever...."
The kingdom of the world has become the kingdom of our
Lord
    and of His Christ,
        and He shall reign forever and ever. (Revelation
        5:12, 13b; 11:15b NIV)

Yes, it is finished!
So is Satan.

That's the message from the moment of His birth.
That's the message of the empty tomb.
Justice has triumphed.
A body of people has been born,
> whose spirits and hearts have been awakened —
>> turned toward the God of love, and truth and justice.

He shall triumph gloriously.
Justice is come upon the earth!!
Remember this when the skies roll dark,
> when the thunder claps,
>> when the foundations of the earth shake.

It *is* finished!
It is finished indeed.
The kingdoms of this earth *have* become the kingdom of our Lord and of His Christ.
Because He lives, you too shall live.
Though it may seem at times that the forces of darkness are
> overcoming the light,
>> that is an illusion.

So, I bring you a paradox:
> the war is won,
>> but the battle continues.

Justice has been done;
> justice is being done;
>> justice will be done.

The Lord God is triumphant.
I know —
> my name is Gabriel;
>> I stand in the presence of God;
>>> **I was there.**

That is why the angels sang at His birth —
> that is why we continue to sing,
>> **"Glory to God in the highest!"**

HOMESICK: MONOLOGUE OF AN ANCIENT HEBREW
1 Kings 8:22-30 (REB)
Psalm 84:1-11a
Ephesians 6:11-18

THEME:
This ancient Hebrew, one of the dispersed Jews, was homesick, not just for his homeland, but for the Temple where the unique presence of God was thought to dwell. His message to us in a time when there is no temple is to let not anything stand in the way of the uplifting privilege of worship.

SETTING FOR THE SERMON MONOLOGUE:
Something is deficient in me. I have never liked poetry any more sophisticated than nursery rhymes. I could have chosen one of the other lectionary texts for the day. In fact, I did include the other Old Testament reading from 1 Kings 8:22-30. All had something of the theme of worship in them. Seldom, however, have I preached from the Psalms — one of the largest books of the Bible. It is my impression that I am not alone. I am quite convinced, however, that in my audience there are many who thrill to poetry. Obviously, the Lord put Psalms there to reach those people. It is literature my congregation needs to be familiar with. It is literature I need to learn to appreciate. Thus, as an exercise in empathy, I tried to see through the poet's eyes — to feel as he felt — to express what I think he wished to express.

HOMESICK: MONOLOGUE OF AN ANCIENT HEBREW
1 Kings 8:22-30
Psalm 84:1-11a
Ephesians 6:11-18

"How lovely is thy dwelling place, O Lord of hosts!
My soul longs, yea, faints for the courts of the Lord;
   my heart and flesh sing for joy to the living God.
Even the sparrow finds a home,
   and the swallow a nest for herself,
      where she may lay her young, at thy altars,
         O Lord of Hosts,
            my King and my God.
Blessed are those who dwell in thy house,
   ever singing thy praise!
      Selah
Blessed are the men whose strength is in thee,
   in whose heart are the highways to Zion.
As they go through the valley of Baca they make it a place of springs;
   the early rain also covers it with pools.
They go from strength to strength;
   the God of gods will be seen in Zion.
O Lord God of hosts, hear my prayer;
   give ear, O God of Jacob!
Behold our shield, O God;
   look upon the face of thine anointed!
For a day in thy courts is better than a thousand elsewhere.
I would rather be a doorkeeper in the house of my God
   than dwell in the tents of wickedness.
For the Lord God is a sun and shield;
   he bestows favor and honor."
(Psalm 84:1-11a, RSV)

My message in that Psalm I quoted has been preserved
   down until your time.

I am its author.
I am pleased that it reverberated in the hearts of my fellow Jews
 exiled to points all over the world ...
  that my words were of such comfort to these exiled people
   that they have preserved them —
    people like myself who longed to go home —
     to be not only in the city of Jerusalem —
      but in the Temple —
       my home.

The Temple, much like your flag is the symbol of the United States of America,
 was the symbol of our nation,
  but it was much more —
It was the seat of the Lord Our God.
The original Temple built by Solomon was a glorious place.
Solomon in all his wisdom built the original edifice
 and it served us well for almost three centuries.
We were so proud.
We loved our God.
We wanted the whole world to know of His glory,
 but especially we wanted the people of Israel —
  those who would make use of it to be reminded of His glory.
Nowhere in the world was there a building so adorned —
 much of it inlaid with gold.
The Temple became a showpiece, coveted —
 lusted after by the kings of many nations.
When Solomon dedicated the Temple,
 Hebrew people came from all over the land to worship that day.
Standing in front of the altar,
 Solomon stretched forth his arms toward heaven,
  in the presence of the whole assembly,
   and prayed:

    1 Kings 8:22-30 (REB)
"Lord God of Israel,

there is no God like you in heaven or on earth beneath,
> keeping covenant with your servants
>> and showing them constant love while they continue faithful to you with all their hearts.

You have kept your promise to your servant David my father;
> by your deeds this day you have fulfilled what you said to him in words.

Now, therefore, Lord God of Israel,
> keep this promise of yours to your servant David my father, when you said,
>> 'You will never want for a man appointed
>>> by me to sit on the throne of Israel,
>>>> if only your sons look to their ways
>>>>> and walk before me as you have done.'

God of Israel, let the promise which you made to your servant David my father be confirmed.

But can God indeed dwell on earth?
Heaven itself,
> the highest heaven,
>> cannot contain you;
>>> how much less this house that I have built!

Yet attend, Lord my God, to the prayer
> and the supplication of your servant;
>> listen to the cry and the prayer
>>> which your servant makes before you this day,
>>>> that your eyes may ever be on this house night and day,
>>>>> this place of which you said,
>>>>>> 'My name will be there.'

Hear your servant when he prays towards this place.
Hear the supplication of your servant and your people Israel when they pray towards this place.
Hear in heaven your dwelling and, when you hear, forgive."

The Temple was the seat of God.
We worshiped Him there.
We made our sacrifices to Him there.
We found our forgiveness there.
It was there that we heard His voice.

The Omnipresent One was not limited to that place, of course.
We knew that.
A crisis occurred in the sixth century B.C. that dramatized that for us.

Sweeping out of the north came hordes of Nebuchadrezzar's Babylonian army.
The army swept away city after city in the foreign nations.
Some of our Israelite people said it was because of their sins,
BUT
"It will never happen here," they said.
We are God's special people.
His temple is in this land.
Then the army swept away the northern ten tribes of Israel.

Again we said,
    "Our northern brothers were sinful and stiff-necked people,"
BUT
"It will never happen here.
The Temple is here.
Yahweh will protect us."
But, in time it not only happened here,
    the temple itself was destroyed,
        and the people of our land were displaced.

The Babylonian king —
    king of Iraq, as you know it,
        Nebuchadrezzar was no fool.
He knew that subjugated people would maintain their nationalistic loyalties.
They would despise any foreign emperor.
They would one day rebel unless he could take their loyalties and frame them around him.
It has always been so.
My people hated the Greek conquerors.
They hated the Roman conquerors in the time of Jesus.
Even in your time, it is so.

The Russian armies dominated their neighbors,
    acquisitioned them,
        formed the Union of Soviet Socialist Republics.
They kept these nations in check,
    formed subject states out of hostile neighbors in places like
    Yugoslavia.
When the Soviet power was weakened,
    those nations declared their independence.
The Serbians, Croatians, and Bosnians are again at one another's throats.
They each refuse to be dominated by the other.
Nationalistic loyalties will always raise their heads in the long run.
Nebuchadrezzar knew that.
However, he had a plan.
He transplanted people like chess pawns.
He took people,
    especially those of the leading families,
        from, for example, Assyria,
            and put them in Lebanon,
                or Palestine,
                    or Phoenicia,
                        or Syria.
He would then take leading families from these countries and move them around also to other lands.
He treated them well.
He gave their sons unusual training;
    he placed them as leaders in their new lands.
Soon they intermarried with the sons and daughters of that land.
They forgot all the loyalties to the nation of their birth.
Their cultures intermingled.
They became like immigrants in the melting pot of America,
    or like Yankees who came for a Florida visit and never left.
The policy worked very well for the most part.

One group of people refused to be assimilated, however.
They were from the two southern tribes of Judea —
    Judah and Benjamin.

Some people still puzzle today over what happened to the northern ten tribes.
They've come up with esoteric fantasies and doctrines built on their speculations —
    weird ideas.
It's almost like those who claim they've seen Elvis.
And of course, some will swear that Hitler is still alive and well,
    at the ripe old age of one hundred plus.
There's no need for these speculations.
It's no mystery.
No, they didn't settle in the British Isles
    (you Anglos are not Jews, though I'm complimented that you want to be),
        nor were they the Indians of North and South America;
            and they weren't the spiritual ancestors of the Mormons.
For the most part, they simply intermingled and intermarried with the people of other cultures,
    or found business in their new land too good to go back to Israel.
They joined the melting pot.
The northern ten tribes never were very loyal to the foundations of Judaism.

But the southern two tribes —
    Judah and Benjamin — were never assimilated.
They refused to follow the ways of Nebuchadrezzar.
They refused to violate their own cultural and religious laws.
They refused to intermarry.
They were loyal to Yaweh.

Seventy years after Nebuchadrezzar carried these Judeans off,
    a new empire and a new emperor, Cyrus of Persia,
        known to you as Iran,
            came to the throne.
He too,
    like Nebuchadrezzar,
        wanted to curry favor with his conquered people.

He sought to do it by reversing the policy of Nebuchadrezzar.
All those who wanted to go to their ancestral home were sent with his blessing —
    whether they were from Phoenicia,
        Lebanon,
            Syria,
                or Judea.

What's the point?
The point is that for seventy years we Jews had no place to worship our God.
Cyrus won our favor by granting us the freedom and substance to rebuild the Temple.
We were grateful,
    even though the glory days were gone.
We were thrilled to have our temple again;
    it was beautiful,
        but when it was dedicated,
            the old men, who had seen the previous temple,
                wept at the contrast.
The Temple lasted almost five hundred years before it was ruined again in battle.
Thank God, Herod rebuilt it —
    At least that old fox did something right during his reign.
There was one humongous problem, however;
    it remains to this day.
In A.D. 70, the Temple was destroyed.
Because of upheavals,
    Jews went to other lands to survive.
Far more Jews lived outside the land than lived in it.
Even today, there are less than five million of us in Israel —
    less than the number of Jews who live in your state of New York.
We Jews who live in exile,
    then or now,
        think of Israel as our home.
We long to be at worship in the Holy City —
    in the Temple.

Ahh, "Blessed are those who dwell in your house ever singing thy praise."
We make pilgrimages at festival times, singing His praises.
This is what my psalm is all about —
    the great desire to be there,
        the planning and fantasy of being there.
Almost like your children anticipate Christmas,
    we fantasized;
        we waited;
            we planned.
No impediment is too great.
We rejoice even when there is great hardship in getting there.
— And when we have to go through the Valley of Baca:
    that is, when we have to cross desert sands in the hot sun,
        no vegetation,
            no water, except the occasional spring or oasis,
                because of our excitement —
                    my passion —
                      their passion —
                          it doesn't seem like a desert.
Indeed, we pilgrims transform this place.
We make springs where there are no springs.
Isn't this what God's children are supposed to do in difficult places?
"Blessed is the man whose strength is in the Lord."
Not only is he blessed,
    but so are those associated with him!
"He goes from strength to strength."
The early rains follow him in the Valley of Baca —
    the desert place —
        a deserted place, where there was almost no water,
            no vegetation,
                an occasional oasis.
But our people,
    as they moved to Jerusalem,
        dug new wells,
            brought in new springs.

They made it alive.
Isn't that what God's people are supposed to do?
Where there is a desert, we bring it alive.

The same wonderful thing happened in your day,
    when Jewish people returned to Palestine in the 1930s, 1940s
        and 1950s,
        Palestine had turned into a desert.
They turned to the Old Testament scriptures,
    and looked where Abraham and Isaac and Jacob dug wells.
They redug those wells.
They irrigated those lands.
They made the desert to blossom as a rose —
    the desert came alive.
They transformed the place.
"Blessed is the man whose strength is in the Lord."
Not only is he blessed, but he blesses those associated with him.
"He goes from strength to strength ...
    The early rains follow him" into the desert place.
We wanted to be in the presence of our people, and our God.

In your time my people, too, crave for a temple.
But there is none.
In 70 A.D., when Herod's temple was destroyed by the Romans —
    only a portion of one wall was left standing and still
    remains —
        we call it the Wailing Wall.
You've seen it on your television sets.
People praying at the wall —
    leaving notes inside its cracks with their prayer requests on
    them —
        like some Christians burn a candle.
Their most important prayers are the prayers for the peace of
Jerusalem.
For the day to come when the Arab and the Jew will live in peace
together —
    when all the world shall live in peace together,
        when the lamb shall lie down with the lion.

We make prayers for the concerns of our own lives.
But most of all,
> we make prayers for the Messiah to come;
>> for His reign on earth —
>>> when the Prince of Peace shall end all strife —
>>>> when all of us shall be at home
>>>>> because of His presence.

Some expect that He will rebuild the Temple on its appointed spot —
That spot is occupied right now by a Muslim sacred,
> holy monument —
>> a mosque called The Dome of the Rock.

Is Messiah's primary concern about a place built out of bricks
> and mortar
>> and stone
>>> and wood?

Or, is He building a people that are called by His name —
> a people of God to worship Him?

Is the mighty presence of Almighty God embodied in human flesh —
Is not the King of Kings and Lord of Lords your temple?
Are the people who worship Him your temple?
Is not your body the temple?
Is that what the scriptures mean —
> that He shall build another place of sacrifice
>> out of rocks and mortar to stand on this spot?

It would thrill me if that were to happen!
> Yet, is that it?

Or is the mighty presence of the living God the temple? —
> His presence embodied in the flesh of the Messiah,
>> King of Kings and Lord of Lords.

That's what we really seek —
> Him and Him alone.

Your Jesus responded to a Samaritan woman, who,
> wondering about the proper place of the temple,
>> asked where the appropriate place to worship the Lord was.

He said, "God is Spirit;
> they that worship him must worship him in spirit and in truth."

It is His presence that counts —
> It is contact with His presence that brings the real thrill.

People seem to worry about where,
> when,
>> and how we should worship.

Some, whom your apostle Paul describes as spiritually "weak,"
> worry about when,
>> where,
>>> and how to worship —

Shall we worship on the seventh day of the week,
> or the first day?

Who cares?

WORSHIP!

Shall we worship at the temple?

That would be delightful,
> but it is important to worship wherever His people are found.

How shall we worship? —
> Formally and quietly,
>> with read prayers and a patterned liturgical service?

Or spontaneously with shouts of joy,
> with dance,
>> with hands raised in the air,
>>> and no printed order of worship?

The answer:

WORSHIP!
WORSHIP THE LORD!

Blessed are they that dwell in the house of the Lord —
> ever singing His praise.

PENTECOST COMMUNION MEDITATION:
MONOLOGUE OF A SAINT
Acts 2:36-47

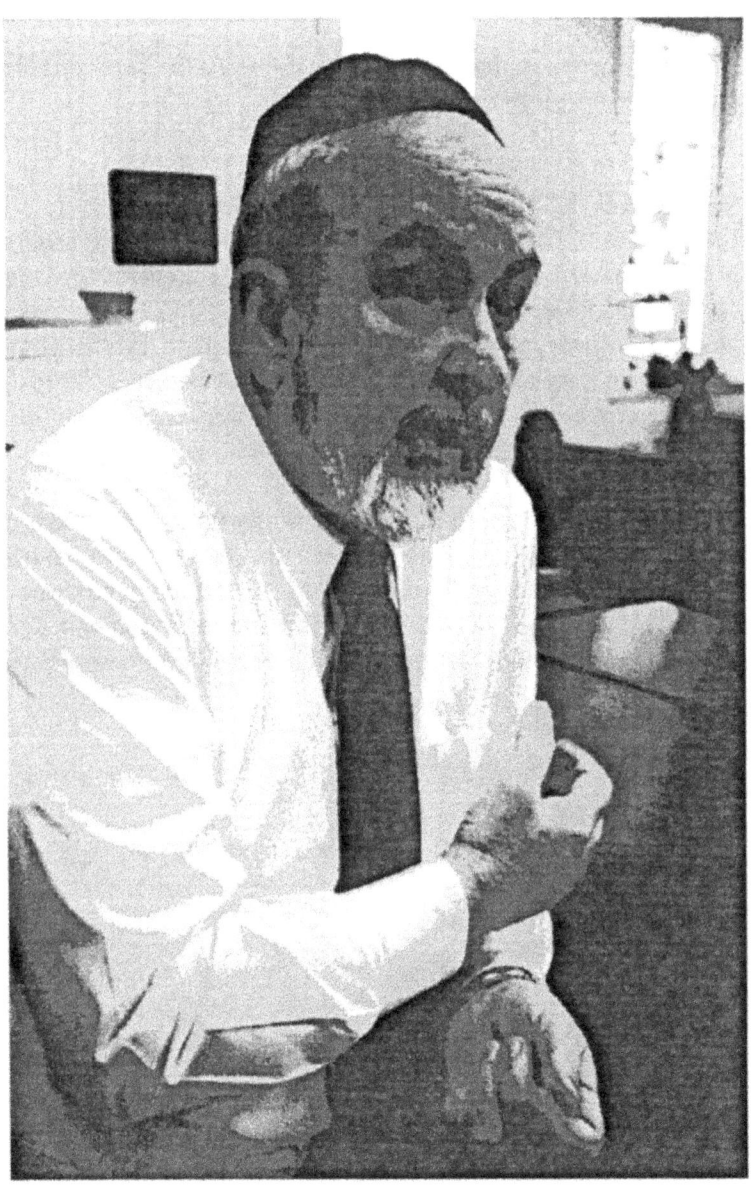

THEME:
The Holy Spirit has, through the years, drawn us to Christ, that He might make us saints and family.

SETTING FOR THE SERMON MONOLOGUE:
Like Abraham, I set out on a journey. After twenty years teaching in a United Methodist Church college setting, I grew restless, but still did not know what to do with the rest of my life. For one year, I took a part-time appointment, a two-church circuit, 65 miles from my home in Lakeland, Florida. I had no idea whether I was up to the task of returning to the pastorate. How does one develop fifty or more sermons a year, and fulfill the duties of a pastor?

Since my first Sunday to preach was in the Pentecost season, it seemed logical to deal with the theme of that season. I also wanted to give the people some idea of who I was. This monologue uses a "glorified" saint, who has been an observer from the beginning, to introduce the Pentecost theme, as well as me — their new pastor.

PENTECOST COMMUNION MEDITATION:
MONOLOGUE OF A SAINT
Acts 2:36-47

I know you were expecting your new pastor, Ed Thorn, to speak this morning,
    but he invited me to come,
        introduce him and his wife,
            and another person as well —
                the person of the Holy Spirit.
Since this is the second Sunday in the season of Pentecost,
    I can speak as a firsthand witness of that event,
        and the days following.

A firsthand witness, you say —
    but that event happened nineteen and one-half centuries ago.
How can you be a firsthand witness?
Don't bother yourself about such details.
After all, with God all things are possible.
Look that up in your scriptures.
Jesus said it.
Saint Paul, in his letter to the Philippian church, the fourth chapter and the thirteenth verse, said it.

Who are you anyway, you ask?
I suppose you mean my name.
Well —
    I'm in the Bible.
I was one of those three thousand people "born again" into the kingdom of God on the day of Pentecost.
My name is not important.
I'm just an ordinary person —
    one of the saints of God.

Oh, I've confused you again, have I?
You didn't think saints were ordinary?

You thought you had to be especially holy or accomplished?
Well, in a way yes,
    and in a way no.
The word saint, *hagios*, does mean "holy one,"
    but I am a saint,
        not because of what I have done,
            but because the Master, in His work on the cross,
                made me holy.

Nope —
    I guess you could say that I had a lot of "ol' Nick" in me.
Why, I remember the time —
    aah, maybe it's just as well that we don't get into that.
That was a long time ago.
But you, too, are saints,
    "holy ones," who have committed your lives to Jesus Christ.
No way, you say —
    no way you are a holy one?
I can practically read your minds.
You are recalling those times when you were less than saintly —
    Someone's thinking about harsh words you've exchanged —
        you and your spouse, huh? —
            Well, again, let's not be too personal.

Let's move on to the first person I wish to tell you about —
    the person of the Holy Spirit —
        the Spirit by whom you were born anew into the Kingdom of God.

The Lord Jesus Christ, in His discourse at the last supper,
    referred to the Spirit five times.
He made it clear that the Holy Spirit was a teacher,
    counselor,
        comforter,
            persuader,
                who would abide with Christ's followers forever.
He will bring to mind those teachings of Jesus His followers have diligently learned.

He will be a counselor to us when we need counseling,
   and He will persuade people who do not know Him
      that Jesus Christ is Lord, whenever the gospel is preached.

I must say,
   when Peter preached the good news to me,
      the words seemed to hit me as if they were coming from
      the very mouth of God —
Indeed, by the convicting power of the Holy Spirit, they were.
He empowered Peter —
   the same man who cowered before the maid in the inn,
      and denied his Lord.
If I hadn't been told that,
   I would never have guessed it.
This man preached with such holy boldness
   that I knew right then and there that I wanted to be a
   follower of the Lord Jesus.
I wept as I thought about the fact that only weeks before,
   when they crucified Him,
      that I shrugged my shoulders and said, "C'est la vie" —
         "Such is life."
I wept too, because I did not avail myself of the opportunity to
know Jesus in the flesh,
   or to hear Him speak —
   to see Him mingle with the people —
      to bless the children —
         and to heal the sick.

The day of Pentecost, however,
   I was born anew by the Holy Spirit,
      and life has never been the same since.
Well —
   obviously I have eternal life,
      or I wouldn't be here.
I've been up there with my Lord all these years.
It seems but a day.
Yes, sir,
   the Holy Spirit is the "great communicator."

And all this time you thought the great communicator was ol'
what's his name —
   you know who I mean —
      former President of yours —
         uhh, Ronald Reagan —
            good man,
               pretty fair president,
but he's like a drop of spit in the ocean compared to the Holy Spirit —
   the One who could put in Peter's mouth the purposes of God,
      who, from all eternity,
         planned to create a community of people who
         would sing and speak of His praises,
            and who had a plan for my life —
Amazing, that this great communicator —
   the Holy Spirit,
      could reach down and touch this spiritually indifferent heart,
         and make me a part of the family of God.
What a community He created!
I'm a son of the living God,
   the Everlasting Father,
      the King of Kings.
You know what that makes me?
Why, I'm a prince —
   a nobody like me!
That's exactly what the Holy Spirit does —
   He communicates, and brings us —
      into community.

Well, anyway, I'm a member of His community —
   the holy community of Christ —
      the church.
What I've been trying to say is,
   that also makes me your brother.

I've been watching you folks from up there in heaven with Jesus,
    and I know you love Him too.
I know you've prayed that the Almighty would send you a minister.
And down there in Lakeland, there was this minister,
    college professor of communication,
        who was beginning to get restless,
            and wondered if there wasn't something more significant he could do in the closing years of his working life.
It was a "cushy" job he had.
You'd be amazed what the Holy Spirit had to do to get him to leave that endeavor.
But the Holy Spirit,
    working through the bureaucracy of the United Methodist Church,
        got you two together.
(That almost took more power than it required to raise Jesus from the dead —
    working through *that* bureaucracy.)

I remember Ed when he was a lad in Ohio —
    born into a Christian home.
His parents took him to church.
Church was a bit of a bore to him as a very young child —
    so much so that one of his earliest memories is that of his mother taking him out of the service,
        down to the basement to give him a paddling.
But, when he was in the first grade,
    a young lady Sunday School teacher,
        who later became his Aunt Dorothy,
            told the story of the crucifixion.
He got a lump in his throat and said aloud,
    "That's a very sad story."
A year or so later, an invitation was given in Sunday School to give one's heart to the Lord —
    and he did.

Then there was a young lady in Indiana,
    some three hundred miles away,
        who was also seeking for meaning in life.
Her older brother became a Christian
    and took her to church with him.
This twelve-year-old young lady became a Christian.
When she was sixteen,
    she moved from Indiana to Ohio.
She started attending the same church that Ed's family had belonged to for three generations.
So the Holy Spirit brought together these two people who had never met,
    and created a new minuscule community.
The first time she laid eyes on him, sitting up there in the choir —
    the Holy Spirit spoke to her and said,
        "That skinny lad —
            (yeah, I know it's hard to believe he was ever skinny)
                that's the young man you are going to marry some day."
Ed never stood a chance.
That's how these two saints,
    Ed and Eldora,
        got together.
Now —
    don't you go worrying about that word "saint" again.
Don't let it scare you.
Ed, especially, isn't always saintly,
    but then God —
        the Holy Spirit,
            and his wife are still working on him.

The number of saints out there are as many as the sands of the sea.
Here you are, saints,
    here in Florida farm country.
You, too, will have the opportunity to sand off some of Ed's rough edges.

All this time you were family —
    even though you didn't know one another.
Now you have been brought together.
We now have communion between some saints of Lakeland and the saints of Lake Lindsey and New Hope.
That's, in part, what we mean when,
    in the Apostles' Creed,
        we talk of the communion of saints.
It is a catholic,
    that is, worldwide, community.
In fact, it is much more —
    it is a communion that surpasses this world —
        it surpasses time and space,
            and binds together, through all time,
                the community of the saints.

One of the ways you communicate your faith,
    and your community with God and one another,
        is in the breaking of bread and the drinking of wine.
You call it communion.
Do you notice that word "communion"?
It's the same word as communicate and community.
They're all one word.
Just as we saints are one —
    drawn together by the Holy Spirit into the community of faith,
    the body of Christ —
        you celebrate your oneness with one another.
You are saints.
You are family —
    some of the Father's many children —
        numerous they are —
            numerous as the sands of the sea.

Let us now celebrate that communion at the table of our Lord.

NUMBER ONE MOTHER
Genesis 2:20-25

THEME:
Adam and Eve speak of our origins. Not only have we all eaten of the "fruit of the tree of good and evil," but we are usually drawn to members of the opposite sex. Yet, while drawn to our opposites, we are also confused by them. They act and communicate differently.

SETTING FOR THE SERMON MONOLOGUE:
This was a mother's day sermon. However, it celebrates God's gift of all women. While we may like to romanticize our mothers, in actuality, they have their foibles. Here Adam is made to share the joys, discoveries, and perplexities of his life with the "mother of all living."

NUMBER ONE MOTHER
Genesis 2:20-25

Good morning, children!
I trust you will not be offended by that diminutive.
When I call you children,
    I am not referring to your age.
I refer to the fact that you *are* all the offspring of me and my wife.
You call her "Eve," meaning "Mother of all living."
That wasn't her name.
It is merely a description.
We didn't really need names at first.
There wasn't anyone else around, after all.
If I talked, she knew I was talking to her.
You, of course, call me "Adam."
That, too, is not so much a name as a description.
Adam simply means "human being."
Since none of you were around back then, I thought I'd share with you some of my perceptions about the very first mother on this "Mother's Day."

About a century ago, Mark Twain,
    I'm sure with his tongue in his cheek,
        claimed he found,
            and translated from hieroglyphics,
                our diaries.
You may find his version in books of Twain's short stories,
    very simply called *The Diaries of Adam and Eve*.

So as I could talk to you today about it,
    I read the biblical book of Genesis.
I also read these diaries.
They refreshed my memory.
Perhaps you find that strange, since I was there.

You older folks should understand how the memory dims a bit over time —
    It's been a few million years since all that happened.

When I read Twain, I found that some of his material wasn't too far off,
    though, at times, he contradicted the Bible.
He also leaves some important material out;
    he doesn't talk at all about our relationship with God.
Twain was a skeptic, you see.
Anyway, I'd like to comment on,
    and share,
        some of what Twain said.
I'd like to correct some of his material.
I'll ignore most of it,
    and I'll add some recollections of my own,
        particularly some of our encounters with God.
I'm glad you folks know our Creator,
    but we encountered Him in a rather unique way.
He used to come down in the cool of the evening.
He walked and talked and shared with us.

Some of what Twain said made light of Eve —
    He was trying to be humorous, of course.
In these politically correct times, however, people have lost a bit of their sense of humor,
    and some of what he says might be offensive to a few of you.
Actually, I don't think Eve would mind Twain's lighthearted exaggeration of her talkativeness.
I may have made some comments along those lines myself, out of exasperation, and lack of experience with her, when she was new.
She and I had an excellent relationship.
There were, however,
    things about her that got on my nerves —
        and, of course, I got on hers —
            but that's another story.

The truth was there were times when both of us thought the other was a bit stupid.
I reckon that's just part of marriage,
    but basically, we loved and respected one another.

Anyway, I did sometimes think Eve was a bit stupid,
    because she chattered on and on in a starry-eyed way a lot.
She often seemed to talk when she didn't have anything to say.
As time went on, however,
    I realized she was not so much sharing content —
        that is, information, with me
            as she was just attempting to relate.
She was that way.
Gender communication research in your time indicates that that's the usual style of womankind.
She was very sociable.
Some of what she said was based on her "woman's intuition" —
    rather than facts and logic.
She was a rather intuitive person.

She, however, also thought I was stupid, at times,
    because I didn't have much to say.
She sort of figured that was because I didn't know anything worth talking about.
Truth is, I didn't exactly go "gaw-gaw" about sunsets,
    the moon,
        butterflies,
            and flowers.
In time, we came to understand that we were just different from each other.
And in time, we came to love that difference.
Actually, right from the beginning,
    I was grateful to God for her.
The Bible records my words when I first saw her.
I burst right into song, singing,
    "This one at last is bone from my bones,
        flesh from my flesh!

> She shall be called woman,
>   for from man was she taken.
> That is why a man leaves his father and mother and attaches himself to his wife and the two become one."
> (Genesis 2:23-24 REB)

We complemented each other very well.
Those differences made her attractive.
She was indeed like a part of me,
   and I a part of her.

She was good and nurturing.
Even in responding to the serpent's temptation there was a bright side.
That sin didn't occur just as a quick whim.
The serpent did tell her she would be like God —
   knowing good from evil.
He made her doubt.
He appealed to her nurturance.
He made her wonder if God hadn't made a couple of mistakes in His creative process —
   a mistake or two that she could rectify.
He made her feel that she could improve on things,
   if given a chance.
Isn't that the way he comes to you?
Generally speaking, do you really intend to do bad,
   or just experiment with some alternatives that may have a "goodly" effect?
So she did some experimenting known to you as "eating from the tree of knowledge."

She did it first, but I, too, responded and ate of that tree.
Immediately, there was a difference.
Whereas, before we wondered if God made some mistakes,
   now we were certain of it —
     Trouble was, we didn't always agree on what needed fixing —
       or if it did, how it ought to be fixed.

We got on each other's nerves.
So did the animals.
They began to attack and even eat one another.

Now, when we ate of that tree, there wasn't any mighty crack of lightning —
    nothing like that.
When she ate, she said, "You know what I'd like to do?
I'd like to go shopping!"

"What's *that*?" I asked, a bit of an edge in my voice.

"I don't know," she said, "but, I want to do it!
I think it has something to do with clothes."

"What are clothes?" I asked.

"I don't know, but I don't like the way you're looking at me,"
she snipped.

"What do you mean?" I asked.

"I mean I feel naked," she said, "and I don't like it.
It's embarrassing!"

I had to admit it was.
I felt like covering up, too, after I ate a bit of that fruit.
So we put our heads together, and came up with the idea to sew some fig leaves together.
We put them on.
"How's that?" I asked.

"Not quite good enough," she said.
    "It won't keep me warm.
        It doesn't really cover me.
            It's all one color.
                It won't last."

On and on she went.
Again, she said, "I want to go shopping."

"Why?" I asked.

"Well, I need something to jazz these clothes up —
    some jewelry maybe,
        or a scarf."

"You don't need any jewelry," I said.
"If we just had Sunday afternoon football," I asserted.

"What's that?
Sounds like something men do when they want to get away from their wives."

I didn't know what it was,
    but I guessed she might be right.
Actually, we thought we might improve on God's handiwork a little.
Now we began to see a lot of deficiencies in God's creation —
    especially in each other.
At last she started wearing a bumper sticker that said, "A woman's place is in the mall."
We were bickering loudly.
The windows were open.
We heard a knock on the door.

"What's that?" we whispered.
Now we were really embarrassed.
We hid.
We didn't want anyone to see us like this —
    half naked and bickering about it.
Who could it be, we thought?
We were the only ones.

Then the knock came again and a voice cried out,
    "Yooooh!

       Yooooh, Adam!
          Yooooh, Eve!"
Then we knew who it was.
We recognized the voice.

God was like that.
He had a charming informality about Him.
He liked to be "cool."
He didn't like to make much of His omnipotence and
omniscience, and all that —
    didn't want to make us feel inferior.
He liked to think of Himself as almost human —
    one of us.
Come to think of it,
    He finally did become one of us, didn't He?
He'd come most evenings for a visit.
We'd walk and talk,
    but this time, we didn't want to see Him.
We were embarrassed.

God knew we were in there,
    so He just pushed his way in, and asked,
        "Why are you hiding?"

"Because we're naked," we said.

"Who told you that?" He asked.
"Have you been eating the forbidden fruit?"

Well, right away, I started blaming the woman.
"The woman gave it to me."
And then I went one step further.
I blamed God.
"The woman *you* gave me, gave it to me."

And Eve, she asked, "Haven't you got anything better for us to wear?"

God gave us some animal skins.
Then He evicted us from the garden to a place where we'd have to work by the sweat of our brow,
> but He hinted at a time when a savior would come and trample on the head of the serpent —
>> ending sin and rebellion.

Things haven't been the same,
> but I love my wife and she loves me.

One day, I went out on a hunting trip.
When I came back, Eve had a new creature.
I didn't quite know what it was.
I had named all the animals,
> and I hadn't seen anything like this.

It made weird noises —
> some of them downright ugly noises —
>> when I tried to sleep.

Eve and the new creature were inseparable, however.
Mostly it just annoyed me.

As time went on, I thought it was a kangaroo.
Its front legs were shorter than its rear ones,
> and it traveled about on all fours with its rump in the air.

So I named it "Caingaroo" —
> Cain for short.

Eve loved it.
I hadn't seen her so happy since we'd been evicted from the garden.
She claimed it was a human.
She even said it looked like me.
I wouldn't know.
I couldn't see myself.
As it grew, however, I perceived that she might be right.
It walked on two legs, and it did talk.

First thing you know, she found another one.
They used to fight and carry on, those young ones.

I remember once I said to Eve,
   "Eve, I know we ate the apple, or whatever fruit that was —
     but these dadblamed kids of ours!"
Eve would have none of that.
She reminded me that there were good times, too,
   when they played well together.
     But good or bad, Eve was content.
She was good with them.
I was happy to see her happy.
We named them Cain and Abel.
I grew to love them as well.

But, sadness came into our lives.
Cain, in a fit of jealousy, killed Abel.
It broke our hearts.
I never wanted to see Cain again.
Eve kept excusing Cain, saying,
   "Cain didn't really understand death.
   He's never seen it before."
I didn't buy that.
She said, "Do you want to lose both sons?"
She was like that.
Understanding —
   and intuitive —
     knowing my heart better than I did myself.

One day she said, "Cain needs a wife."

"What's that?" I asked.

"A female partner,
   just like you've got," she replied.

"But, we're the only ones," I said, rather annoyed.
"Where will you get one?"

"I don't know, but he needs one,
   and I'll ask God and we'll get him one!"

"You're crazy," I said.
"I'm going hunting."

When I came back Cain had a wife.
Where did she get her?
Skeptical people have been asking the question ever since.
Whenever I'd ask her, she'd just smile mysteriously, and say,
   "God provides."

God made Eve for a helpmeet for me.
I'll never quite understand her, but I'm glad He gave her to me —
   Bone of my bones,
   Flesh of my flesh.
She's the Number One Mother.

IT'S HELL, I SAY: HEROD SPEAKS
Matthew 2:1-12

THEME:
I regret the insensitive way I spent my life. I do wish for you to understand me, through my times and the culture that shaped me and my decisions.

SETTING FOR THE SERMON MONOLOGUE:
The sermon was used on the first Sunday after Epiphany. Epiphany is the season that recognizes the first revelation of Christ to the Gentiles (Magi). Whereas, in Advent we look forward to the coming of Christ, Epiphany is also the time that we contemplate His coming, and ask what our response to Him ought to be.

For this reason, I have chosen Herod as one who has had much time to look back and contemplate how he responded, and how that response might have been different.

ORAL STYLE SENTENCES THAT MAY NEED CLARIFICATION:
1. Page 89: "The bowing, scraping, smiling, obsequious people ..." is rambling, yet gets across what otherwise might require several sentences to communicate. The following sentence on a "different point of view" is saying in shorthand that my (Herod's) perspective is that anyone who saw things differently was evil.
2. Page 92: "Essential deaths." In oral style, and increasingly in written style, the essence is made clear and more dynamic without saying, "I, of course, thought these deaths were all essential." Similarly, "Loyal to Caesar" abbreviates the sentence of "I was loyal to Caesar."
3. Page 97: "Regret, regret, regret," uses a kind of parallelism to escape the prodigious task of an extended elaboration on the psychological status of Herod's hell. In terms of Marshall McLuhan it is "cool." It says much while saying little.

IT'S HELL, I SAY: HEROD SPEAKS
Matthew 2:1-12

It's hell —
   hell, I say.
It's hell to know that I wasted my life.
I didn't think so at the time.
I thought I was something.
Others seemed to think I was something, too.
The bowing,
   scraping,
     smiling,
        obsequious people
           rarely gave a hint in my presence of anything but
           adoration and respect.
Out of my presence, I knew there was another element —
   a different point of view —
     evil ones, I thought.

Respect is something I coveted.
I was appointed by Caesar himself to overcome the Hasmoneans,
   earlier called the Maccabees.
This group dominated the intertestamental period —
   between the close of the Old Testament and the opening of
   the New Testament.
They led insurrections against the Greeks, and established
Israel's relative independence,
   until Pompeii brought them under the Roman yoke in 63 B.C.

The Jews were, for the most part, an intolerant bunch.
Certainly, there were those who allied themselves with Rome,
   but they were a scant minority, except for those who lived
   outside of Israel.
They considered the Gentiles (Roman soldiers) unclean.
They refused to accept Roman rule.
They began to overemphasize aspects of their religious ritual.

For example, Roman guards throughout the empire carried imperial standards.
These were poles that bore the Roman insignia at the top.
These standards would, at times, touch off riots among the pious Jews.
They took them to be a violation of the commandment to make no graven image.
They even forbade the use of coins that bore the emperor's portrait.
You Christians —
    you have the same commandments —
Do you object to the coins and postage stamps in your pocket that have an image of people your nation wishes to honor?
A side issue for me, from a first century perspective, is — I do wonder about your culture —
    is the best you have to honor on postage stamps Marilyn Monroe and Elvis Presley?
Do you not have family portraits hanging on the wall of your home?
Do you understand the kind of narrow-mindedness I had to deal with?

Secondly, even if you do object to graven images,
    is there not a place for tolerance of differences?
You should have seen the squabble that occurred when I allowed Gentiles to erect statues of myself.
I guess I'm not a good Jew.
Perhaps if I had made more of an attempt to understand these stiff-necked people,
    I would have modified my approach.
Maybe then I could have been more successful.
They certainly were an obstinate bunch,
    but then I thought that as their appointed leader, they should just do as I said —
        follow my authority without question.
We were not into this "democracy thing."
It became a power conflict.

I ruled by fear and cunning.
Of necessity, it was not important that these Jews love me —
    only respect me.

The problem with that, I have discovered, in my eternal place of contemplation,
    is whenever decisions are imposed —
        when they are not owned by the people whom they affect,
            the people will seek to undermine the authority of
            those who imposed these decrees.

You might not understand the fact that I tried —
    I tried —
        to win their loyalty,
            while simultaneously trying to maintain my position with Rome
                and the Gentile culture it represented —
                    not to mention my Gentile constituents.
I was not reared as a typical Jew —
    and these Hebrew people never let me forget it.
I was an Idumean,
    a descendant of Esau,
        Jacob's, that is, Israel's, twin brother.
We were neighbors of the Judeans.
As a result of their conquest of our territory, we were forced to become Jews —
    outwardly.
In actuality, the sibling rivalry that commenced in the lifetime of Jacob and Esau has never ceased.
Even in your day, there is strong conflict between their descendants.

As part of my attempt to be a good Roman, I created gymnasiums, sponsored athletic events.
I underwrote the Olympic games in Greece and was named "Perpetual President" of those Olympic games.
I believed this competition was good for the people,

but my fellow Jews got all hung up on the lack of clothing
worn by the athletes.
I built a large theater and a hippodrome for chariot races in the
city of Jerusalem,
and an amphitheater in the hills nearby.
This, too, they scorned.
I rebuilt the fallen walls of the city of Jerusalem.
And, I built the Temple in Jerusalem.
It was a temple that even the ancient Jewish historian, Josephus,
described as
"magnificence never surpassed."
The cost was incalculable.
Did it win me love?
No!
Honor?
No!

Someplace along the way, I gave up trying to win their love,
but I did maintain, if not love —
if not respect —
then fear.
I maintained order.
In spite of all I did, history,
indeed, your biblical narrative,
has not treated me well.
The focus has often been on the assassinations I ordered —
all ordered to maintain the peace.
It is almost impossible for you to understand the chaos that
would have been prevalent in that part of the world had I not
been strong —
had I not been willing to make tough decisions.
Yes, I killed my brother-in-law.
I killed all the Hasmonean claimants to the throne.
Essential deaths.
Yes, I killed even my wife, Marianne, and her mother.
Of all my wives, she was my favorite,
but she too was a Hasmonean.

In time, I suspected her loyalty.
I also had reason to think she might have had an adulterous relationship with my Uncle Joseph.
It seemed reasonable to execute him as well.
I was not one to let my emotions get in the way of my duty.

You've heard that Augustus Caesar is quoted as having said,
    "I would sooner be Herod's pig, than his son."
That's easy for him to say, sitting in his ivory tower in Rome.
He sent me here to clean up this rebellious mess —
    and clean it up I did,
        regardless of my personal loyalties.
Two of my sons I killed because there was a rumor that they were plotting against me.
Maybe they did —
    maybe they didn't,
        but they were the sons of my beloved wife, Marianne,
        the Hasmonean princess.
As long as they were alive, the Hasmonean dream of a Jewish empire was still there.
I couldn't risk it.
You understand, I did this to keep the peace.
It was fitting that a few should die,
    that the blood of many might not be spilt in the skirmishes and uprisings.
One other of my sons I killed shortly before my death —
    though not Hasmonean, he seemed to be "ambitious."
Then of course, there were numerous minor would-be Messiahs that had to be,
    shall we euphemistically say,
        "neutralized."
At the time, this seemed to be the right thing to do.
Bloodthirsty —
    no —
        just looking after "number one" —
            and, of course, loyal to Caesar —
                yes, loyal to Caesar.
It was my job to maintain the peace.

In the last year of my life,
    nearly as I can recollect,
        three astrologers, Zoroastrian priests of Persia,
            presented themselves to me.
Though they were men of high standing,
    I might not have given them audience, were it not for the fact
    that they sought the King of the Israelites,
        the recently born Messiah.
They came there to my palace because they assumed any new heir would be my offspring.
I inquired of the chief priests at the temple I built for the Jews, where the Messiah was to be born.
Bethlehem, they said —
    according to scriptures, Bethlehem.
I asked the Magi to return and bring me word when they found him.
I intended to kill the child.
But, they never returned.

I was alarmed.
Alarmed, yes.
You say,
    but you were an old man.
Why be alarmed?
You had already ruled 36 years.
Why did you care?
Why did you want to kill him?
What possible threat was he?
Were you protecting your sons?
No way!
I was doing my duty, as I saw it.
He was but one more potential rabble-rouser in a long line of them.
I was, after all, the Palestinian arm of Caesar.

In retrospect, how limited my perspective was!
Since I could not find out who he was,

    I ordered all male babes, under two years of age, in the
        Bethlehem area, executed.
How was I to know?
Bethlehem is a small area, I reasoned.
Only a handful would die.
It is fitting that a few should die to prevent the death of the many.
Many of these babes were born to the poor —
    to families that already had too many mouths to feed.
I thought of myself as doing a righteous thing.
It was merely a method of population control.
I, who killed my own sons, certainly was not hesitant to slay the sons of another.
I didn't even shed a tear.
How could I know?
I was sheltered from all that.
I was reared to think in terms of power —
    not to think in terms of others.
I had no ability to comprehend.
I never heard the screams of these mothers.
Had I heard them,
    I'm still not sure I would have understood.
They were rabble —
        not quite human.
I had no more concern than you might have if you trapped a rat.
Vermin!
That's what they were to me.

I had heard an old wives' tale that when one dies, his life flashes before his eyes.
That cut no ice with me.
I had no reason to think I was less than perfect.
You imagine that we tyrants are some sort of evil plotters.
Not really.
Not as I know myself, or others like me.
I would imagine that the Pharaohs,
    the Hitlers, etc.,
        were just like me.
We thought we were doing good!

A narcissist like me can't comprehend any morality that is concerned with the common good,
    unless it is also good for the ruling class.
What was good for Herod the Great was good for all my adherents.

As I lay dying, however, my life did pass before me —
    like a judgment of God —
        gentle, but oh so firm and certain.
For the first time, I "heard" the screams of the bereaved.
I felt the sorrow of those I had hurt.
I felt the sadness of the poor, who bore the brunt of the taxation that built the monuments to myself throughout Palestine.
Their offspring —
  even one single child —
    meant more to them than all theaters,
      amphitheaters,
        hippodromes,
          athletic contests,
            and royal palaces in the whole of the Roman empire.
Those taxes I took could have fed,
  clothed,
    and nurtured their young ones.

I have a different perspective now —
  but it's too late.
Too late, it is, to pass on to my sons and their sons' sons
  the knowledge of what really matters.
My tiny empire was split up among three of my sons —
One of them,
  my son Herod Antipas,
    was responsible for the death of John the Baptist.
Jesus Himself appeared before him on the eve of His death.
It was he —
  my son and his men —
    that mocked Him,
      put on Him a royal robe,
        and sent Him back to Pilate for judgment.

On it goes.
It's the system.
Perhaps I could have made a difference.
Maybe not a big one,
    but one in my small area of the world —
        and a difference in my family.
It's hell.
Regret,
    regret,
        regret.
That's hell.
I see it now, but I can't repair the past.

The future can be different —
    not because of me,
        but because of you —
            the spiritual descendants of the One whose life I almost snuffed out.
                the One my heir might have saved.

This Child's kingdom was not one of force,
    deceit,
        and power.
In my own time,
    I scorned any other kind.
This Child's kingdom was not a threat.
I know that now.
    I know —
        know and regret —
To you, however,
    the Savior has been revealed —
        Learn of him!
Make him your Lord.

POOLSIDE BLESSING: MONOLOGUE OF A PARALYTIC
John 5:2-16

THEME:
We sometimes follow routines that are a substitute for a living. Instead of having a life of our own, we give up and become passive. In fact, that passivity can be a deceptive and manipulative style of control. Jesus' question to the paralytic by the pool was, "Do you want to be healed?" Do you want to get a life, or is life as you now live it a means of avoidance and control that you find too comfortable to give up?

SETTING FOR THE SERMON MONOLOGUE:
The scripture is a lectionary reading. How does it feel to be a paralytic with little hope of being healed, and to find yourself singled out by an unknown healer with a challenge?

POOLSIDE BLESSING:
MONOLOGUE OF A PARALYTIC
John 5:2-16

Thirty-eight years I lay beside that pool.
Each morning friends or family members brought me there.
I think they wanted me to be healed more than I myself did —
    if for no other reason than having to transport me there.
They were the ones who had to care for me —
    feed me,
        bathe me.
I could not care for myself.

So, why did they trouble themselves to take me daily to the pool of Bethesda,
    since it was just one more chore?
The pool of Bethesda is like your Shrine of Lourdes in France.
All sorts of people went there,
    the blind,
        the lame,
            the deaf.
We went there because there was a tradition that when an angel troubled the water,
    the first person in the water would be healed.
What do I mean by an angel troubling the water?
Well, we didn't actually see an angel —
    though some claimed they did.
What we saw was a bubbling up of the water —
    almost as though the water had come to a boil.
When that happened,
    all the sick dashed to the pool like a thundering herd.
In your time, people who know about these things have a simple explanation for that bubbling.
They speak of underground springs erupting.
Who is to say?
That certainly removes all the mystery.

The fact was that, still, people were healed.
Ah yes, you in your modern wisdom say,
   "But those were psychosomatic illnesses" —
      some of you might even explain the healings by your
      Savior that way.
There may be some truth in what you say,
   but it seems to me that your scientific explanations are often
   as simplistic as our own primitive Hebrew explanations.
Who cares?
The author of all healing is the Creator —
   Let's not lose sight of that.
Even when you go to a modern physician,
   and she or he gives you a pill,
      or performs surgery,
         it isn't the physician that healed you.
That physician was only acting in concert with the laws of God,
   who is the source of all healing.
Thank God for them,
   but physicians are only the Almighty's assistants.

Anyway, I was waiting there one day —
   like any other day.
As John's gospel reports,
   a whole multitude of sick people were there as always —
      waiting,
         just waiting.
The question was —
   who would be first in the pool?
Alas, it was never me.
In all those years of waiting,
   it was never me —
      never,
         never,
            never.
It was distressing.

Then, on this particular sabbath day,
> this fellow I took to be a rabbi and His entourage happened by.

There were lots of people there,
> but He ignored all the others.

Walking up to me, He says,
> "Do you want to be healed?"

"What kind of nut is this?" says I to myself.
> "Do I want to be healed?

Why in thunder do you think I lie here?"
But, I hold my tongue, and simply say,
> "Sir, I have no man to put me into the pool when the water is stirred up.

While I am inching up to the pool on my elbows,
> someone else beats me to the waters.

It's futile!"
You see where my faith was placed —
> not in the God of gods,
>> but in the water.

Actually, I guess I really didn't answer His question!
I offered an excuse.

But, Jesus faced me very abruptly with a reality I don't think I ever dealt with.
Did I really *want* to be healed?
I hadn't thought of it in that way before.
Most of us have a lot of ambivalence about things.
As time went by, I had become almost comfortable with my impairment.
Perhaps I didn't have some of the freedoms others have —
> perhaps I couldn't even care for myself.
>> But there were advantages —
>>> neither did anyone demand anything of me.

I had no responsibility for myself —
> and certainly not for others.

Indeed, others waited on me —
> I was in their debt,
>> but I also had their attention.

John Bradshaw, a former candidate for the priesthood
    and a psychologist,
        who in your time does extensive counseling,
            writing, and lecturing,
                especially before twelve-step groups,
                    in his book *Creating Love,* tells of the power of
                    being ill physically or mentally.
Sometimes he will have three people out of a large group act mentally ill.
No one knows who those role players are.
Eventually he calls the three up on the platform and interviews them.
When he asks how they felt,
    they usually say, "Powerful!"
There is a sense in which our helplessness can put us in control
That can be difficult indeed to relinquish.

Within me I knew,
    and the Savior knew,
        that I needed to make a decision.
But, before I could say anything,
    He gave me an order that I willingly obeyed.
"Rise up," he said,
    "take up your bed and walk."
I did it.
I walked.
I carried my pallet.
I couldn't believe it.
I felt life in my legs.
I could stand on them —
    I could, and did, move them.
After 38 years as a paraplegic,
    I could walk.
I felt absolute hilarity.

Since it was the sabbath day,
    my first stop was at the temple.

There,
> of all places,
>> I assumed I would find those who would rejoice with me,
>>> and praise our God.

But, before I even got there, some religious people,
> many of whom knew me,
>> got all upset because I was carrying my pallet —
>>> no bigger than one of your sleeping bags —
>>>> on the sabbath day.

I was bewildered —
> confused.

Why were they not happy?
Why did they observe that tiny violation of their law and get angry?
Why did they focus on that, instead of the miracle in their midst?

Maybe they were like me, before Jesus came along.
We get so used to operating in certain ways —
> routines —
>> and even assume that God Almighty has to act according to our routines.

When we see that the Lord has wondrous ways of working —
> far beyond our imagination,
>> and He calls us to expressions of faith,
>>> it can be very threatening.

It's a risk!
But, the rewards outweigh the risks.
"Do you want to be healed?" He is asking.
Or are you interested in following your routine?
Are you ready to come out of your comfortable places and follow a God who is infinite? —
> Whose dreams for you are not limited to man's petty concepts?

It's scary, I know.
I'm thrilled that He challenged me.
I'm thrilled to be made whole.
Rejoice with me!
His ways are wonderful.

Rejoice with me in the words of the Psalmist: (Psalm 8 RSV)
> O Lord, our Lord, how majestic is thy name in all
> the earth! Thou whose glory above the heavens is
> chanted
> by the mouth of babes and infants, thou hast
> founded a bulwark because of thy foes,
> to still the enemy and the avenger.
> When I look at thy heavens, the work of thy
> fingers, the moon and the stars which thou hast
> established;
> what is man that thou art mindful of him,
> and the son of man that thou dost care for him?
> Yet thou hast made him little less than God, and
> dost crown him with glory and honor.
> Thou hast given him dominion over the works of
> thy hands; thou hast put all things under his feet,
> all sheep and oxen, and also the beasts of the field,
> the birds of the air, and the fish of the sea,
> whatever passes along the paths of the sea.
> O Lord, our Lord, how majestic is thy name in all
> the earth!

I AM ZACCHAEUS
Luke 19:1-10

THEME:
Zacchaeus was a man who loved power, wealth, and status. As a tax collector, however, he was shunned by polite society. Inwardly, he had not found satisfaction in his accumulation of wealth. Whatever it was that made him climb a tree to see Jesus, he found what his inward man longed for.

SETTING FOR THE SERMON MONOLOGUE:
Zacchaeus is in the lectionary readings. He is a fascinating little man about whom children sing. He can tell his own story better than I can preach about him.

I AM ZACCHAEUS
Luke 19:1-10

Hello?
Surprised to see me?
Yes, I am Zacchaeus.
You don't look happy to see me.
Please don't close the door!

You're right.
I was here just last month —
    and collected a tidy sum then, didn't I?
No —
    No!
I'm not here to bleed more money out of you.
In fact, I bring this gift of bread,
    dates,
        and goat milk.

Wait!
Wait!
Don't refuse my gift —
    Don't close the door —
        Haven't you noticed I didn't bring the Roman guard with me?
Ah yes —
    you have noticed,
        and that's why you had the nerve to close the door on me.

You don't want my gift?
You don't think of me as a friend?
You don't want to have anything to do with me?
I can't say that I blame you.
You have every right to feel that way.

What's the trick?
No trick.

See —
    nothing up my sleeve.
I've come to offer an apology.

No! No! —
    Now hear me out.
You are right;
    something more is due you than an apology —
        That's why I brought the dates,
            the goat milk,
                and the bread.

Oh, you misunderstand.
No, I realize that's not adequate compensation for what I've done to you.
I offer you your money back.
What's the catch?
None.

Fat chance?
Chance of a snowball in hell?
Please —
    please don't make epithets about my ancestors.
They weren't curs.
In fact, they were good orthodox people.
It's my fault —
    not theirs.
I forgive you for those remarks,
    and again I say, I don't blame you.

Here take this —
    count it.
Ah yes —
    Do you believe me to be sincere now?
Ah, you have noticed that there is a little extra in there, have you? —
    As a matter of fact, four times as much as I took from you.

You're astounded?

So am I!
I cannot believe I am doing this.
And you —
    you are just one of many.
I hope not all people will doubt me as much as you —
    but then, who knows —
        maybe some will even spit in my face.
Actually, you are gracious considering —

Did I get religion, you ask?
Well, yes —
    in a manner of speaking, I did —
        but it isn't quite that simple.

Sure —
    yes —
        I'll come in and sit.
Let me tell you my story.

I'm not quite sure where to begin.
You know my value system.
You know the kind of person I am —
    that is, I was.

I guess I was always greedy.
I saw, even as a child, the power that belongs to the wealthy.
I was determined to get my share of it —
    and maybe a little more.

I grew up in this city of Jericho —
    a city with a rich history, as you know —
        the city miraculously conquered by our ancestors under
        the leadership of Joshua,
            after they completed their desert wanderings.

This beautiful garden of paradise was later given to Cleopatra by
Anthony.
I suppose you know that, too.

When I was growing up,
    I used to pass the palace of Archalaus,
        Herod's son.
His rose gardens perfumed the air.
That was in marked contrast with the stench of the squatters'
huts, where I grew up.
I made a vow.
Someday —
    someday, I would work for Caesar —
        the one who made it all possible for Herod and Archalaus.
I, too, would be rich and powerful.
That's all I dreamed of.
I was prepared to pay the cost —
    but —
        I can't say I enjoyed being in a crowd
            and hearing people mumble curses under their breath
            about me.
Sometimes, when my back was turned,
    they even spit on me.
When I would turn around to see who did it,
    all faces were blank with innocence —
        as though they neither saw nor did anything.
They treated me like a common criminal —
    an outcast;
        like a robber,
            a cutthroat,
                a brothel-keeper.
The more they did so,
    the heavier I made their taxes.
I got even —
    after a fashion —
I did feel lonely at times,
    but, I loved the power.

I started out as a small-time tax collector.
I outbid everyone else,
    particularly those with a conscience.
I got the job.
Others said I bid too much in that auction,
    that I couldn't possibly make any money.
They just didn't know how ruthless I could be.
I made sure that I always had a good contingent of the Roman army with me when I went out to collect taxes.
I stopped at nothing.
What did I care if some widow had nothing left to buy groceries —
    scourge of the earth, anyway.
        Right?
If she was a widow,
    there was probably a curse on her.

I could have gone on living like this forever,
    but something caught my attention recently.
When going into some few houses,
    they invited me in and treated me with respect —
        like an ordinary, real person.
Finally, I asked one of these families why they did this —
    They said it was because of some carpenter turned rabbi —
        Jesus of Nazareth.
They shared with me how He turned their lives around.
His teachings, they said, were unusual —
    "He taught us to love," they said.
"But, it was more than His teachings.
He seemed to exude the aura of the God of Abraham,
    whose son I am.
He forgave sin.
He healed the sick and the broken-hearted.
He could bring peace —
    shalom — to His people."

I began to wonder.
What good is all my ill-gotten wealth, if everyone hates me,
    if I at last find myself in Hades?
Here I was at this point.
I had risen to the position of chief tax collector.
I had it all.
I became one of the richest men in all Jericho.
I was going up the ladder,
    yet inside, I felt empty.

One day, I heard that Jesus was coming here to Jericho.
I determined to see Him.
Alas, when I got there, the streets were crowded.
Unfortunately, I am short of stature, obviously,
    and I couldn't see him —
        I spied a sycamore tree, however —
            Without thinking, I shinnied up that tree.
Can you believe that —
    fat, little old man that I am?

Almost before I saw Him, He saw me —
    He called me by name —
How He knew me, I do not know —
"Zach," He said,
    "Come down, I'm going to lunch with you today at your
        house."

I couldn't believe it.
Apparently, others couldn't either;
    they kept murmuring, "He's a friend of tax collectors
        and sinners."
Thank God He is.
His acceptance of me has made a difference, not only for me,
    but for those very murmurers.
My values have been reversed.
Whereas I coveted the outward things,
I now crave the inward.

I wanted the material —
    now, I want the spiritual.
I treated people like things for my own gratification —
    now, I see them as persons.
Formerly, I felt disconnected from everyone.
Now I feel connected,
    even to my Maker.

Just yesterday, I heard the Mrs. talking to a neighbor about what happened —
    how, at first, she was annoyed because I brought guests home for dinner
        without warning her in advance —
            how, in the midst of the meal,
                I turned to the Savior and again repeated my vow,
                    "Half of all I have, I give to the poor.
                    If I have defrauded any person,
                        I'll restore it four-fold."

"Then, Jesus said to him the sweetest words I ever heard —
    'Today, salvation is come to this house.' "
And the little woman said,
    "You know, I don't think we'll be eating so high on the hog anymore,
        but, I believe things are going to be better around this house.
    Why, this morning, he even took the garbage out!"
I laughed right out loud.
If I had followed the orthodox teachings of my family,
    we wouldn't be eating hog anyway.
But, she's right.
I may even have to give up my vocation.
I'll probably be a lousy tax collector.
I'm not into control anymore.
I've surrendered the control over my life, and its circumstances,
to the Master.

I found myself,
   wonder of wonders,
      entering this relationship without even negotiating a contract.
My old self would have bargained with Jesus.
You know how I am.
I use pressure.
I'm like a used-car salesman —
   uhh, I mean used-camel merchant —
My new self simply surrendered.

What's that you say?
You'd like to know Jesus, too?
He's nearby —
   still at my house —
      teaching other sinners.
Come over for supper,
   I'll introduce you to Him.
Shalom, y'all.

A Postscript: According to one tradition that cannot be verified, Zacchaeus became a bishop of Caesarea.

REUBEN: I'M NOT A SANDWICH
Genesis 37:19-34

THEME:
Reuben is one of the forgotten characters of the Bible — the one who, by normal processes, should have received the birthright as the firstborn son of Israel. He tells of the common experience of feeling like a second-class son, because Israel favored Joseph. He shares family events, as well as his inner soul.

SETTING FOR THE SERMON MONOLOGUE:
Most persons have heard the story of Joseph and his brothers. Many people have heard the story over and over. They have rarely, if ever, heard the perspective of any of the brothers. There are two sides to every story.

REUBEN: I'M NOT A SANDWICH
Genesis 37:19-34

My name is not a common one in your society.
The only place you seem to use it is not for one of your sons,
   but for a sandwich made of Jewish rye,
      kosher corned beef,
         and sauerkraut.
If you haven't guessed my name by now, it's because you don't
have many delicatessens in Perry farm country.
My name is Reuben.

There's a tongue-in-cheek saying among some of you modern
people that God gives us the firstborn child for practice.
When the rest of the children come,
   the firstborn experimental model should be thrown away.
As a firstborn of Israel,
   otherwise known as Jacob,
      I should have been the favored one —
         but I was not.
I should have received the birthright.
I did not.
I was never quite sure why.
Perhaps it was because I was born to Leah,
   Jacob's first wife —
      fraudulently given to him by my grandfather Laban.
When she came to him late on his wedding night she was veiled.
It was dark.
My father had imbibed in the fruit of the vine.
He thought she was his beloved Rachel.
She was the wrong woman.
Thus, the marriage,
   based on fraud,
      didn't impress my father,
         nor apparently could I win his favor.

Maybe it was the fact that my father purloined the birthright
from his slightly older twin brother Esau,
    that he attempted to justify his own chicanery by selecting
    the next to youngest child —
        Joseph —
            as his favorite,
                instead of following the tradition of our society.
Maybe that was why I was not favored.
My father was a rebel.
He didn't take kindly to following rules laid down by someone
else, based on tradition.

Joseph is such a favorite with you Christians
    that you may have trouble identifying with my brothers and
    me.
Likely enough,
    until this moment,
        most of you haven't heard of me —
            or for that matter, you don't know much about my
            other brothers,
                Judah,
                    Simeon,
                        Benjamin,
                            Dan, etc.,
                      but you do know Joseph.
He has always gotten all the attention.
Undoubtedly, there is good reason —
    given his lofty position as an Egyptian administrator.
But —
    you didn't have to live with him!
He was insufferable!
We felt like second-class sons.
When he was seventeen years old, Dad sent him out to work
with us tending the flocks.
He went home telling tales about us —
    tales that made him look good and us look bad —
        he was a tattler.

Do you know what it's like to live with a spoiled teenager
   who seemed to think himself better that the rest of us?
He didn't have the responsibilities the rest of us had.
Dad made him a special coat with long sleeves that indicated he
was the favorite.
The rest of us wore sleeveless garments.
He lost no opportunity to pompously parade around in that coat.
Then there were those crazy dreams.
He could pat himself on the back better than a contortionist.
He seemed to think he was God's gift to us.
We thought he was a bungle from heaven.
The tattletale, with special status, began to tell us his dreams —
   dreams that made it clear he thought he was someone special.
For example,
   he dreamed that all of us were out in the fields,
      binding sheaves.
Suddenly,
   his sheaf stood upright,
      and ours bowed down to his.
Besides him,
   there were eleven of us brothers, right?
So —
   what's that tell you,
      when in a second dream, the sun,
         moon,
           and eleven stars bowed down to him?

Our father, Israel, actually pondered the dreams as a possible
prophecy.
We didn't see a prophecy.
What we saw was a lust for power that meant he wanted to lord
it over us —
   that he wished for the birthright that not only gave him a
   greater share of the inheritance,
      but also made him head of the clan.
In no way were we prepared to accept that brat's leadership.

Even if his dreams were legitimately of God,
> he would have done well to know that even a whale only gets harpooned when he spouts off.

The next time our father sent him out to check up on us,
> we were still furious!

When we saw him in the distance,
> some of my brothers wanted to kill him.

"We'll dispose of his body in one of the cisterns," they said.
"Then, we'll see what comes of his dreams."
I suggested a compromise —
> that we put him in a cistern,
>> but that we shed no blood.

Later, I intended to rescue him —
> not, mind you, because I liked him any more than my brothers did.

In fact, if anyone stood to gain something,
> it was I.

I was the normal recipient of the birthright.
But, I was generally straight.
I was a typical firstborn.
Maybe it is because the firstborn tends to be more straight,
> more experienced,
>> and responsible that the tradition of the birthright,
>>> with its leadership provision, was normally given to the firstborn.

I don't know.
My father never quite viewed me, though, as stable.
He never forgot —
> he could not forget —
>> that in a weak moment I slept with one of his concubines, Bilbah.

It seemed to him that I wished to usurp his power.
Nonetheless, I alone,
> among the brothers,
>> would not have killed Joseph.*

I respected,
   yes, even loved,
      my father too much to allow him to suffer such injury and
      hurt.
Yet, Dad called me "unstable as water."
I leave to you to decide for yourself who was the most stable.

Unfortunately,
   or fortunately,
      depending how one views the "accidents" of history,
         some Ishmaelite and Midianite traders happened by.
My brother Judah suggested that instead of killing "Joey,"
   that they sell him to the traders as a slave.
Had I been there at that moment, that would not have happened,
   but I was tending to other responsibilities.
That's the way with us firstborn.
We work while others play, or make mischief.
The brothers took Joseph's robe,
   tore it,
      and bloodied it with animal blood.
They showed it to our father, Israel,
   who mourned
      and wept profusely —
         I never had the heart to tell him —
            and I was no tattletale.
It was better left alone.

Again, fortunately or unfortunately,
   the story did not end there.
Unfortunately, I say,
   like many of our sins,
      they have a way of coming to light and embarrassing us.
But years later when Father found out Joseph was alive,
   he was so delighted that he forgave us —
      at least after a fashion.
I never did regain his favor.
More importantly, though,
   Joseph forgave us.

In retrospect,
    I can see that we were like the pig in the old Russian proverb
in which the pig said to the horse,
      "Your feet are crooked;
          your hair is good for nothing."
It's easier to judge others than it is to examine our own deficiencies.

We all had something to learn.
I hope our father learned something about showing such gross favoritism toward one brother over the others.
We brothers learned that all of our plotting and animosity did nothing to enhance our position.
It only broke an old man's heart.
And, Joseph?
He had a lot to learn, too.
He learned it well.
A more magnanimous heart I have never seen.

More than a decade passed since we sold Joseph.
We heard nothing of him.
Outwardly, life went on much the same as it always had.
For years, Joseph's face would appear in my dreams —
    and I felt guilty —
        guilty because I didn't find an adequate way to put a stop to it.
We used to talk about it out under the stars as we sat on the hillsides tending our flocks.
My dreams were mild compared to the nightmares of some of my brothers.
They were haunted by the look of horror on Joseph's face,
    as his brothers collected their money from the Ishmaelites who shackled him —
      the look on his face,
         and the tears as he kept looking over his shoulders —
           the look of unreality at the brothers —
His face seemed to say, "Surely, this is a bad joke —

Surely, you're going to come and release me."
    But they didn't.

We were haunted also by my father's tears.
We argued.
Oh, how we argued through the years about whether he really deserved such a severe fate.
We argued over who was more responsible for what had happened to him.
We kept waiting for the other shoe to drop.

Finally, it did.
A severe famine struck the whole area.
Our crops didn't grow.
Our sheep didn't fatten.
Their wool lacked luster.
At times, we thought that we ourselves may have caused the wrath of Almighty God to come down upon us,
    and the entire region.
Surely not —
    but we wondered.
In the time of famine,
    Father sent us to Egypt to buy grain —
        the only group of people around us who foresaw the famine,
            and prepared for it by warehousing the grain,
                under the leadership of none other than our visionary brother, Joseph.
There, at the government market, we ran into a bearded man,
    an Egyptian in his early thirties,
        who greeted us harshly, and accused us of being spies.
He threatened, through an interpreter,
    to arrest us.
Again we argued with one another —
    argued in Hebrew, our own language,
        that we were in this pickle —
            kosher pickle of course —
                because of what we had done to Joseph.

I said to my brothers,
    "Did I not warn you not to do wrong to the boy?
        But you would not listen."
Surely none of the Egyptians could understand us.
The interpreter who knew Hebrew
    was paying no attention,
        since we ceased talking to the young Egyptian official.
It seemed, though, that the official was listening —
    can you listen with your eyes?
If one can, he did —
    sad eyes, that he dabbed at, as though to prevent a tear from
    rolling down his cheek,
        as he turned his back —
            and went out.
Suffice it to say, he tried us in a variety of ways —
    held Simeon in prison, until we should return with our
    youngest brother, Benjamin, to validate our story —
        Benjamin, who now was given the status formerly thrust
        on Joseph.

On the second trip, he made a captive of Benjamin —
    swearing that he was a thief —
        that he had stolen the Egyptian's silver cup.
Benjamin, the only other child of our father's beloved wife
Rachel —
    the one she gave birth to as she died.
This was too much.
Judah offered his life in exchange —
    telling him of the old man's grief —
        telling him that would bring the old man down to his
        grave.
The administrator began weeping.
He ordered all his assistants out.
"Out!
    Out!" he said.
His next words terrified us.

He announced in Hebrew,
    "I am Joseph."
He had grown older, and was changed in his appearance.
He previously had talked only in Egyptian.
We did not suspect that this man of immense status could possibly know us.
We were speechless —
    struck so dumb we could not answer his simplest questions.
We thought we were goners, until he said,
    "Do not be distressed.
    When you sold me as a slave into Egypt, you meant it for evil,
        but God meant it for good ...
    He has made me ruler of all Egypt.
    There are yet five years left of the famine.
    Go bring our father and your families and reside here."

When Pharaoh heard it, he bestowed great gifts upon us because of Joseph.
We settled in Egypt.
The family that we, by our own jealousy,
    thoughtlessness,
        and evil deeds, tore apart,
            God put back together.
We had to learn to forgive —
    all of us.
Jacob and Joseph forgave us.
We forgave Joseph.
None of us —
    except possibly Benjamin,
        who was too young to be involved,
           were without blame,
                but isn't it wonderful that the God of gods that we worship,
                    and you worship,
                        can take the blackest of things and bring good out of it?

Blessed be the name of the God of Abraham, Isaac and Jacob, whom you and I worship.
In His eyes, we are all the firstborn.
May you have a double portion of His grace.
May all of your blackest nights be followed by the brightest dawns.

BOAZ: I AM BLESSED!
Ruth 3:1-5; 4:13-17

THEME:
Our God uses traditions to bless, but He isn't stuck in them. He will even bypass normal traditions when it will accomplish His purposes.

SETTING FOR THE SERMON MONOLOGUE:
On two successive Sundays in the fall of 1994, the Old Testament lectionary reading was from the book of Ruth. In the first one, I extolled Naomi. The message title was "How's Your Mother-In-Law?" It centered on the need to recognize people seldom recognized. In a sense, the book of Ruth is about her. It is principally, however, about another woman, Ruth. I believed I could talk about her better by allowing her husband Boaz to tell this story — a story of love, and a story of an unlikely Midianite woman who became the grandmother of King David.

BOAZ: I AM BLESSED!
Ruth 3:1-5; 4:13-17

Blessed be the God and Father of Abraham,
   Isaac,
      and Jacob,
         Father of us all.
I am an unusually privileged man.
Some of my blessings are obvious to all who know me.
I own substantial lands.
I have wealth and power,
   but all these things pale in comparison to the sense of contentment He has given me.

You know me,
   strangely enough,
      as the husband of Ruth.
Weird!
You've heard that we were a patriarchal society.
Women in our society were usually known for their spouses.
I, on the other hand, am known to you because of my *wife*.
Probably it is true that we were a patriarchal society.
We didn't have the labor-saving devices that you have that enable a woman to do the work of a man.
Women stayed home, bore our children —
   often many children.
We were responsible for heavy labor,
   for the administration of family and community affairs outside the home.
But the ladies were treated well,
   honored and loved.
They were given a place in our history.
Two of the books of the Bible are named after women —
   Ruth and Esther.
Without Esther, there would have been a great slaughter of Israelites.

Some of our other historical books speak of the heritage we have
through the women of Israel — Miriam, Moses' sister; Deborah,
  who slew an enemy king; Samuel's mother,
    who gave us one of our greatest prophets; and Rahab, the one
    who made possible the conquest of Jericho.

I was fortunate enough to be married to Ruth the Moabitess.
She, like Rahab, is one of the two foreign women who are
featured in the line of famous women of Israel,
  who were not Israelites.
That, in itself, is remarkable —
  we were a clannish people.
Over and over, our priests and prophets warned against
  intermarriage with foreign women.
Certainly there was a strong element of racism in our society,
  but this was not the God-given reason for such prohibitions.
We believed that our children should marry those who shared
our faith —
  who had similar values.
Marriage is a difficult thing.
Your Saint Paul said,
  "Be not unequally yoked with unbelievers."
These were women of faith, however.
That is the essential difference.
To look merely at their ethnic background,
  and reject the person on that basis alone,
    is to miss God's blessing,
      provision,
        and opportunity.
He isn't just the God of Israel,
  as some of my contemporaries thought.
The love and faithfulness of Ruth, the Moabitess, enabled
        Yahweh,
  not only to bless her mother-in-law, Naomi,
    but to do dramatic things for Israel,
      indeed, all humankind.
God works in unusual ways.

The tale is a tender one.
Ruth and her mother-in-law, Naomi, were widows.
Ruth, out of loyalty to Naomi,
    left her family and homeland
        to settle with her in Israel.
That's how I came to know her.

It was the time of the barley harvest.
In your culture,
    you talk about the seasons of the year,
        spring,
            summer,
                fall,
                    and winter.
We were more likely to designate the times of the year with
regard to a kind of crop,
    that is, grain planting time,
        the time for hoeing flax,
            the time for the barley harvest,
                or for tending the vines.

Anyway, by some strange "coincidence,"
    she came to glean grain in my fields.
I say "coincidence."
It's been my experience that when someone is praying, as Naomi
and Ruth were,
    coincidences take place.
Anyway, it was the custom,
   indeed the law of the land,
       that the poor,
           the widows,
               the orphans,
                   the handicapped,
                       be allowed to come behind the hired
                       hands to glean grain they left over.
We didn't have a government agency,
    no health and welfare department,
        no food stamps —

The poor survived by whatever small jobs they could secure,
   or by begging,
      and by gleaning in the fields,
         that is, to pick up the leftover grain.

I noticed her right away,
   and asked the foreman of the harvesters who she was.
She was different.
She didn't look like some of the chronic poor.
She was different in her bearing.
You would call her middle-class.
She was a very hard worker —
   full of energy.

My workers told me the story of how she came to Israel with Naomi, her mother-in-law,
   to take care of her after the deaths of their husbands.
Naomi's deceased husband, Elimelech,
   was a near kinsman of mine.
I felt a warmth for such a one as that, who looked after her.
I ordered the men not to harass,
   embarrass,
      or touch her.
Indeed, I asked them to let some stalks of grain drop deliberately,
   that she might pick them up.
I fed her lunch at the end of that day.

After she threshed it, she had nearly three fourths of a bushel of grain to take home.
Ruth was naive, but Naomi knew that someone had taken notice of her.
"It was a man named Boaz," Ruth said.
"He told me not to glean elsewhere,
   but to stay with his workers, where I would be safe."

"Wonderful!" exclaimed Naomi.
"He is one of our kinsman redeemers."

"He is a — what?"

"A kinsman redeemer.
When a man dies leaving no heir,
   a close relative is expected to buy any land,
      take care of the widow,
         and have a male child by her.
That way the family name survives,
   and the widows are cared for.
The land then reverts back to the child upon the death of the kinsman redeemer.
Put on your best clothes tonight.
Watch where he threshes.
Note where he lies down after eating and drinking.
Uncover his feet.
He will tell you what to do."

That night after we worked hard,
   I ate a good meal,
      had plenty of wine to drink.
I was feeling merry.
I lay down and slept.
In the middle of the night,
   I was startled to find her lying at my feet.
I asked what she was doing there.
She replied that she wanted me to act as her kinsman redeemer.
I was surprised.
I was an old fellow compared to her.
I was a contemporary, after all, with her father-in-law, Elimelech.
"May the Lord bless you," I exclaimed.
"You haven't run after the young men —
   either rich or poor.
You've come to me?
I'll do what you ask.
All my townspeople speak of your noble character.

There is one relative,
    closer than I,
        who has the first right.
I'll speak with him before this day is over."

I filled her shawl with grain for Naomi, and I set off for town at dawn.
I went to the town gate.
When the kinsman redeemer came along,
    I told him of the property that was for sale by Naomi.

"I'll buy it," he said.
"Okay, are you aware that Ruth goes with it —
    that when you die,
        the land will not go to your sons,
            but to Ruth's sons to provide for her and Naomi if she yet lives?"
"Whoa!!
That would endanger my own estate.
I don't need family problems like that," he gasped.

"Then give me your sandal in the presence of these elders,"
I said.
"They will be witnesses to the abdication of your rights."

You may think that's a strange thing to do.
When the man gave away his sandal,
    it was a seal of his intention.
You make out papers in front of a notary or a lawyer,
    file the deed papers with the courts.
We had a simpler system.
A man gave away his shoe to the other one to whom he transferred his rights —
    in the presence of eyewitnesses.
The system worked.
I became the husband of Ruth.

That is my claim to fame —
   not my own achievement —
      but as her husband —
You know the rest.
She had a son, Obed,
   the father of Jesse,
      father of David the shepherd king.
That means also that the Messiah,
   your Jesus,
      is one of my descendants.
That means that David the King had the blood of an outcast
Moabite coursing through his veins.

How blessed I am.

Blessed be the father of Abraham, Isaac, Jacob, and Jesus the Christ.
How majestic are thy ways, oh Lord!
"But, as it is written,
   Eye has not seen,
      nor ear heard,
         nor has the heart of man conceived,
            the things God has prepared for those who love him." (1 Corinthians 2:9)

         Our God is awesome!

JOSIAH SPEAKS:
AN ANCIENT KING BRINGS GREETINGS
2 Chronicles 34:8-14, 29-33

THEME:
The Temple was restored after years of decay — even desecration. The remodeling that took place on a physical level, however, is symbolic of a need also to rebuild our lives.

SETTING FOR THE MONOLOGUE SERMON:
After worshiping in the present building since 1917, this 126-year-old congregation needed to remodel. There were serious structural problems, not to mention several aesthetic concerns. The church was out of the sanctuary for over six months. The sermon was for a time of celebration and reconsecration of building and people.

JOSIAH SPEAKS:
AN ANCIENT KING BRINGS GREETINGS
2 Chronicles 34:8-14, 29-33

You are not the first to be concerned about the restoration of your place to worship,
    as you well know.
I, Josiah, King of Jerusalem, bring you greetings from my people.
We found the need to refurbish our temple in my time,
    some 26 centuries ago.
I commend you for your work,
    your sacrifice,
        and your vision to serve the people of this community.
I'm sure this beautiful place is special to you
    and has many memories
        and traditions behind it.

Our Temple, likewise, was important to us.
It was the center, not only of our nation's worship,
    it was also the center
        and symbol of our nation.
It was for us the place where Yahweh Himself uniquely dwelt at the altar
    in the Ark of the Covenant,
        in the Holy of Holies.
The Temple was patterned after the tabernacle used in the wilderness,
    the plan of which was given to Moses under the inspiration of our God.
Now we were no longer a nomadic people,
    but a settled people.
David, our greatest king,
    a shepherd,
        warrior,
            hymn writer,
                and lover of God,

          gathered the material for a more permanent place of
          worship three millennia ago.
His son Solomon built it.
It was the most beautiful building in all the world in its day.
Skilled workers and the best of materials were imported from all over.
The interior walls were covered with cedar and cypress,
    much of which in turn was overlaid with gold.
In the vestibule up front were bronze pillars,
    forty feet tall
        and twenty feet in circumference.
Many of the furnishings were made of gold.
Even the hinges and door handles were made of gold.
In the room we called the Holy of Holies,
    the nails were made of gold.

However, within a century we fell on hard times.
First there was a civil war.
One strong nation became two weaker ones.
Then there were the enemies from without.
More and more we became vulnerable to them.
Our rulers sought ways to buy them off.
Money was borrowed from the temple treasury.
Money that should have gone to the repair of the Temple was used instead for a form of national defense.

One of the big threats to us that never quite became a reality was the Scythians.
They gobbled up several of the nations around us.
You know them as Russians.
As with your nation
    the Russians were a threat to us for almost another century.
They were, however, but one of many.
Preparations for possible warfare can drain the resources of a nation.
In time Assyrians,
    known to you as Iraqis,
        swooped down,

and gobbled up the northern ten tribes of Israel
that split off from us during the reign of King
Solomon's son,
Rehoboam.
My great-grandfather, Hezekiah, was on the throne at the time the Assyrians defeated the northern Jewish kingdom.
He prevented an outright war between our southern kingdom and Assyria by paying them off.
We became their subjects.
You think you have taxes!
My great-grandfather, Hezekiah, was a good and godly king,
    but he felt he had no choice but to strip the gold and silver from both his palace
        and the Temple.
Even that did not fully satisfy Sennacharib, King of Assyria,
    but he did not attack us.

King Hezekiah, whose very name meant "Yahweh is my strength,"
    made such reforms as he could in cleansing our nation from paganism.
He was, however, followed to the throne by his son,
    my grandfather, Manasseh,
        who was wicked and idolatrous.
Grandfather systematically set out to undo the reforms of his father Hezekiah.

To please the Assyrian masters,
    he adopted their gods.
He reveled in Assyrian sovereignty,
    and of course was handsomely rewarded for that cooperation with these pagan perverts.
He worshiped the sun,
    the moon,
        the stars,
            Baal and Ashterof.
He even followed their ritual of child sacrifice
    and filled Jerusalem with innocent blood.

He sacrificially burned his own son to appease these gods,
    who lived only in pagan fantasy;
        and he gave a pagan name to my father — Amon.
I hate to admit it,
    but these times under the rulership of my grandfather,
        Manasseh, were, until that time,
            perhaps the darkest moments of our nation's history.

At age 22 my father Amon succeeded him
    and did nothing to bring reform.
After only two years as king,
    he was murdered by a servant.
I was left an orphan.
At the age of eight I became king.
I was under the tutelage of Hilkiah, the high priest.
It is a terrible loss to give up one's father at such a tender age,
    but it was a great gain to be under the tutelage of Hilkiah
        and his fellow priests.

The priests of the temple of Yahweh took no chances with me.
I was tutored by them,
    instructed in the ways of the God of Abraham,
        Isaac,
           Jacob,
                Moses,
                      David,
                          and Hezekiah.
I was able to perceive that He alone is God.
He alone is worthy of worship.
In a sense, even my name is prophetic.
In your language it means "healed by God."
Certainly, I found His healing touch,
    and our nation, Israel, found healing.
In the eighth year of my reign, I sought after Him.
I soon began a purge of Judah and Jerusalem.
The altars to Baal we tore down,
    but the real effort began in the eighteenth year of my reign
        when I sent Shaphan and Joah to repair the Temple.

They hired men with money given by the faithful people,
> not just from Judah
>> and Benjamin,
>>> but even from the people of Manassah,
>>>> Ephraim and all the remnant of Israel that so long
>>>> ago had separated themselves from us to form a
>>>> new nation.

The workers laid new stone where it was broken,
> and installed timber for beams and joists where they had
> fallen down.

But the real magical moment came —
> ahh, such a delightful memory —
>> when Hilkiah the high priest found a scroll in some dark
>> corner of the ruins and proclaimed,
>>> "I have found the Book of the Law!"

The Book of the Law —
> so long forgotten.

We had sired a generation,
> a nation that no longer even paid lip service to that law.

Indeed, when it was read to me, I was astounded,
> confused,
>> and bewildered.

I had little or no idea of either its promises or its curses.
I tore my clothes and wept before Almighty God.
I ordered the sacrifices of children to the pagan god Molech stopped.
Wizards,
> sorcerers,
>> and sacred prostitutes I put out of business.

My people restored the Temple.
Bulls,
> goats,
>> and lambs were sacrificed once more on the altars to
>> Yahweh,
>>> our God.

We rededicated our Temple,
    and we celebrated.
We celebrated
    and we worshiped!
Singers and musicians found their appointed places.
It was a splendid time.

What I am saying, I suppose,
    is that this was not just a dedication of mortar,
        wood,
            stone,
                and precious metals.
It was so much more.
It was a restoration of memories of yesteryear,
    but even that was not the best of it.
It was a renewal of the vision of the people of God to our values,
    our spiritual heritage,
        and a rededication of our lives to the One who created,
            redeems,
                and sustains us.

May these days be all that and more to you
    as you consecrate this place of worship.
The blessing and promises of the God of Abraham,
    Jacob,
        and David,
            in whose tradition you stand,
                be upon you
                    and all who worship in this holy place.

    Amen.

SECTION II

**Standard Format Sermons
That Include Monologues
As Illustrative Material**

INTRODUCTION TO SECTION II

If Marshall McLuhan is right, we have a generation of people, many of whom do not think in a linear, logical, propositional mode. Yet, there are many who do. In the average parish, there is also a generation that wants the logical mode. How do we serve them both?

First, as appealing as monologues are, they are the exception rather than the rule. I personally use a monologue only every four to six weeks. It may be that in some liturgical churches, there will be people who consider the monologue as inconsistent with the style of worship. In those situations, the monologue might be reserved for special occasions, such as an evening banquet. If done within the formal service, one might wish to choose a monologue that is quite serious in format.

Second, monologues can be incorporated within the standard sermon as illustrative material. Storytelling has always been appropriate, and well accepted. The tendency is for people of most any generation to remember the illustrative material long after they have forgotten the sermon itself. A monologue can be another means of presenting illustrative material.

Some will argue that people don't need illustrations. They need principles to live by. Yet, almost any minister is aware that she or he spends time counseling persons who are quite familiar with gospel principles, but don't know how to apply the abstract principle to their specific situation. Stories hold attention, in part, because they take the abstract and make it concrete. People see themselves in the characters of the stories. Mark Galli and Craig Larson (*Preaching That Connects*, Zondervan, Grand Rapids, Michigan, 1994, pp. 42, 47) claim that

> *One television journalist associated with the highly popular* 60 Minutes *says the producers never do a story about an issue unless they can find a person to tie that story to....*

Journalists want to communicate truth, but we soon realize that effective articles are more than words logically arranged. An article that is read — the only kind worth writing — must have clear writing about a fresh subject, but it must also touch the human heart, addressing some kind of human concern.

There is no need for either/or thinking with regard to linear, propositional sermons versus monologues and other forms of storytelling. It is both/and. The fact that good monologues have a theme, or central idea, means that monologues are not anti-linear in thinking. The traditional linear sermon may — indeed, to be effective across generations, must — contain stories or monologues. Whichever is done should attempt to reach both the left and right brain. Monologues provide one option to be heard. The well-illustrated traditional linear sermon can also do that, provided it has a dramatic flair that helps to resolve the central proposition or issue involved.

JESUS IS ALIVE AND WELL
Luke 24:13-35

Jesus is alive and well.
I know, for I saw Jesus face to face.
No, it wasn't some magical, mystical vision.
I saw her in the little inner-city Eloise United Methodist Church
of which I was part-time pastor in the mid-1980s.
The congregation was so minuscule, she would have been almost
impossible to miss.
She was a "country-girl" type, petite with blond hair —
    age 36.
Her smile was contagious,
    in spite of the terrible burden of tragedy that haunted her.

Annie was born on the wrong side of the tracks to a large,
    poor,
        and dysfunctional family.
She married very early —
    perhaps to escape that setting.
She soon had a son,
    followed shortly by a daughter.
The man she married was a good and decent fellow,
    but for whatever reason,
        the marriage eventually fell apart.
The children she bore were lovely,
    intelligent,
        and well-behaved.
She was a great mother.

Someplace along the line Ann met the Master,
    and a young man named Steve as well.
As a Florida Southern College business major,
    Steve worked part-time to fill the Eloise pulpit for two years
    preceding me.
Together, the family developed an unusually close walk with the Christ.

She was the youth group counselor and Sunday School teacher.
Young people took to her like ducks to water.
When Steve graduated from Florida Southern College,
    he got a great position as a stockbroker with Merrill Lynch,
        but they continued to worship in the Eloise church.
Their future was extremely bright —
    or so it seemed.
Almost simultaneously with Steve's graduation,
    Annie's beloved sixteen-year-old daughter Vicki
        was killed in a head-on wreck.
That was just six weeks before I became pastor.
Yet, for weeks, I knew nothing about it.
Certainly, nothing in Annie's bearing indicated to me her deep sorrow.

In spite of a full-time job running her own business,
    Ann was very involved in the church,
        and in the community as a volunteer.
Some of her work I was totally unaware of until almost a year after I left Eloise.
Mark Rivera, the president of Anchor House Ministries,
    a Christian residence for troubled and delinquent boys,
        told me that she voluntarily cut the hair of the boys who resided there.
You see, she was a beautician.
She owned her own shop,
    a block from the Winter Haven, Florida, mall.
She named the shop "Transformation."
She felt herself to be like a caterpillar,
    transformed into a butterfly because of her relationship with Jesus Christ.
She was a simple kind of person that drew people to herself.
Out of those encounters,
    she wanted to become a part in their transformation inwardly,
        as well as outwardly.
When her clients would ask about the strange name for her shop,
    she would launch into her transformation story.

Then one day in my first months at Eloise,
> her younger brother was killed by a railroad train as he was walking along the tracks —
>> the second close member of her family to die within a period of months.

If her faith faltered, one would never know it.
However, her mother-in-law found these words written on a sheet of paper in Annie's Bible,
> and gave them to me after Ann's own death.
>> "How long does it take for a mother's heart to heal? Probably a lifetime."

Outwardly things were fine in spite of tragedy,
> but inwardly she was hurting and bruised.

One day, months after the death of her daughter, Annie visited the grave site.
It was hot —
> like it can be in the summer months in Florida.

When she parked her car she, therefore, left the windows down a ways.
She put her purse on the seat and walked over to the tombstone to pray.
A teenage boy came by, reached in, and stole her purse.
Ann ran after him, yelling.
A guard noticed them and also gave chase.
The lad dropped the purse.
After the guard went home, the young man came back.
Most of us would have had harsh words for him —
> not Annie.

She struck up a conversation,
> told him about her daughter Vicki,
>> and she told the fellow that Jesus loved him.

Then, in her own sweet way, she prayed aloud for him before she left.

Just before the following Christmas —
> a bit after the first anniversary of Vicki's death,
>> Ann asked me to pray for her.

She wasn't feeling well.
Her shop was very busy during the holiday season.
She didn't want to disappoint any of her customers.
As a result, she didn't take off to see a physician.
When she did,
    it was too late.

I loved Annie and Steve deeply.
Until that time, I had never loved and lost anyone who meant so much to me.
I wasn't alone.
When people heard of her cancer,
    hardly any of our members missed church.
Never have I seen so much prayer go up for one person.
The little church was much fuller than usual, as people came and prayed for her.
All around, people talked of her works —
    love, benevolence —
        They prayed.
One man made a vow that he would fast until he knew she was healed.
I, personally, thought of little else.
I also fasted and prayed on several days,
    off and on for weeks.

How could it be God's will that one so young and good —
    who had so much love to give
        that she gave so freely — could die?
Die while yet in her mid-thirties.
Before Easter, I preached her funeral.
Annie Springer was dead at the tender age of 37,
    leaving many heartbroken friends and loved ones.

I never in my life came so close to a breakdown.
My faith was sorely tried.
In some ways, it has taken years for me to recover.

I wondered how such goodness and productivity could disappear,
> while evil and destructiveness never seem to terminate.

I particularly wondered why my prayers, and the earnest prayers
of so many people, seemingly had no effect.

Where was the authority that I and others have —
> authority Jesus delegated to us when He said,
>> "Ask whatever you will in my name and it shall be done
>> for you."

One day I'm going to ask the Almighty about that question.
That may be, in fact, the very first question I ask of Him when I
get to the other side.

You may remember that Job, too,
> in that ancient Old Testament writing,
>> angrily shook his fist in the face of his Creator,
>>> asking questions.

He got an answer eventually —
> yet it was no answer.

When the Almighty finally spoke it was only to ask a question of
Job (38:4, 12, 32).
> "Answer me [Job]: "Where were you when I laid the earth's
> foundation?
>
> Tell me if you understand ...
>
> Have you ever given orders to the morning,
>> or shown the dawn its place? ...
>
> Can you bring forth the constellations in their season?"

I understand very well why the two persons on their way to
Emmaus were sad as they walked the seven miles from
Jerusalem on that early Easter A.M.

With a very sad heart, they pondered the loss of their
33-year-old friend.

They pondered the rumors they heard from other friends —
> friends who, because of their great loss,
>> were so saddened that they seemed to be hallucinating.

Even when Jesus appeared to them, and explained from the
scriptures,

       beginning with Moses and down through all the prophets,
          why the Christ had to suffer these things to enter His
             glory, they were kept from recognizing Him.
It was only as He came into their house,
      sat down at the table opposite them,
          and broke bread in the familiar way,
             that they recognized Him.
Then He disappeared.

At that time, the rejuvenated couple returned at once, the seven miles to Jerusalem,
      and added their witness of His resurrection.

This story, with different characters,
      was repeated over and over in the weeks after Easter —
          disciples in despair and fear —
             He appears —
                they scarcely can believe their eyes.
Then, just before the Feast of Pentecost,
      He ascended into heaven to sit at the right hand of the Father.

The world so often appears to us as though it is going to hell in a handbasket —
      especially as we read the morning papers,
          or view the evening news.
The resurrection of Christ says loudly and clearly that,
      though evil will exist until the end of time as we know it,
          the Almighty knows what He is doing.
He is active.
He is doing His work.
Now He incarnates Himself in believers.
We become the body of Christ in our times,
      as we allow Him to live in us.

Look around you.
There is evil in this world.
No doubt about it.

There is even evil in us to the extent that we do not follow Him.
Look around again, though.
Take a second look —
   even a third and fourth look —
      and you will see acts of mercy,
         acts of goodness,
            even acts of self-sacrifice done in the name of
            Christ.

Because He lives,
   we live.
Because He lives,
   I saw Him in the person of Annie Springer,
      and my life was enormously enriched.
Because He lives, others will see Him in you,
   for sometimes, He comes to us as He did to his disciples,
      and we don't even recognize Him.
Lutheran minister Walter Wangerin speaks of this in his parable
The Ragman.

   Even before the dawn one Friday morning I noticed a
   young man,
      handsome and strong,
         walking the alleys of the City.
   He was pulling an old cart filled with clothes both bright
   and new,
      and he was calling in a clear voice:
         "Rags!"

   "Rags!
   New rags for old!
   I take your tired rags!
   Rags!"

   "Now this is a wonder," I thought to myself,
      for the man stood six-feet-four,
         and his arms were like tree limbs,

        hard and muscular,
            and his eyes flashed intelligence.
Could he find no better job than this,
    to be a ragman in the inner city?

I followed him.
My curiosity drove me.

Soon the Ragman saw a woman sitting on her back
porch.
She was sobbing into her handkerchief,
    sighing,
        and shedding a thousand tears.
Her shoulders shook.
Her heart was breaking.

The Ragman stopped his cart.
Quietly he walked to the woman.

"Give me your rags," he said so gently,
    "and I'll give you another."

He slipped the handkerchief from her eyes.
She looked up,
    and he laid across her palm a linen cloth so clean and
    new that it shined.

Then, as he began to pull his cart again,
    the Ragman did a strange thing:
        he put her stained, snotty handkerchief to his own
        face;
            and then he began to weep,
                to sob as grievously as she had done,
                    his shoulders shaking.
Yet she was left behind without a tear.

"This is a wonder," I breathed to myself,
    and I followed.

"Rags!
Rags!
New rags for old!"

In a little while, the Ragman came upon a girl whose head was wrapped in a bandage,
   whose eyes were empty.
Blood soaked her bandage.
A single line of blood ran down her cheek.

Now the tall Ragman looked upon this child with pity,
   and he drew a lovely yellow bonnet from his cart.

"Give me your rag," he said,
   "and I'll give you mine."

The child could only gaze at him while he loosened the bandage,
   removed it,
      and tied it to his own head.
The bonnet he set on hers.
And I gasped at what I saw:
   for with the bandage went the wound!
Against his brow it ran a darker, more substantial blood —
   his own!

"Rags!
Rags!
I take old rags!" cried the sobbing,
   bleeding,
      strong,
         intelligent Ragman.
"Are you going to work?" he asked a man who leaned against a telephone pole.
The man shook his head.

"Do you have a job?"

"Are you crazy?" sneered the other.
He pulled away from the pole,
   revealing the right sleeve of his jacket.
It was flat,
   the cuff stuffed into the pocket.
He had no arm.

"So," said the Ragman.
"Give me your jacket,
   and I'll give you mine."

Such quiet authority in his voice!
The one-armed man took off his jacket.
So did the Ragman —
   and I trembled at what I saw:
      for the Ragman's arm stayed in his jacket,
         and when the other put it on,
            then he had two good arms,
               thick as tree limbs;
                  but the Ragman had only one.

"Go to work," he said.

After that he saw a drunk, lying unconscious beneath an army blanket,
   an old man.
He took that blanket and wrapped it round himself,
   but for the drunk he left a new suit of clothes.
The Ragman was weeping uncontrollably,
   and bleeding freely at his forehead,
      pulling his cart with one arm,
         stumbling for drunkenness,
           falling again and again,
              exhausted,
                old,
                   old and sick.

I wept to see the change in this man.
I hurt to see his sorrow.

The little old Ragman —
   he came to a landfill.
He came to a garbage dump.
He sighed.
He lay down.
He pillowed his head on a handkerchief and a jacket.
He covered his bones with an army blanket.
And he died.

Oh how I cried to witness that death!
I slumped in a junked car and wailed and mourned as one who has no hope —
   because I had come to love the Ragman.
Every other face had faded in the wonder of this man,
   and I cherished him;
      but he died.
I cried myself to sleep.

I did not know —
   how could I know? —
      that I slept through Friday night
         and Saturday and its night, too.

But then, on Sunday morning, I was wakened by a violence.
Light —
   pure, hard, demanding light —
      slammed against my sour face,
         and I blinked,
            and I looked,
               and I saw the last
                  and the first wonder of all.
There was the Ragman,
   folding the blanket most carefully,

        a scar on his forehead,
            but alive.
And, besides that, healthy!
There was no sign of sorrow nor of age,
    and all the rags that he had gathered shined for
    cleanliness.

Well, then I lowered my head and,
    trembling for all I had seen,
        I myself walked up to the Ragman.
I told him my name with shame,
    for I was a sorry figure next to him.
Then I took off all my clothes in that place,
    and I said to him with dear yearning in my voice:
        "Dress me."

He dressed me.
My Lord, he put new rags on me,
    and I am a wonder beside him.
The Ragman,
    The Ragman,
        the Christ!

THE END OF BABEL
Genesis 11:1-9
Acts 2:1-12

The time of Pentecost was a joyous one in the lives of the Jewish people.
In contrast to Passover, where they ate unleavened bread to commemorate the solemn passage out of Egyptian slavery,
> they baked yeast bread of the first harvest of grain of the new growing season.

The feast of Pentecost always occurred on Sunday, fifty days after Passover.
Jewish pilgrims came from all over the world to be in the holy city for that celebration.

Jesus died during Passover.
He, however, came alive,
> conversed with His disciples,
>> and ascended into heaven shortly before the Feast of Pentecost.

He spoke to them of the Holy Spirit,
> whom He would send in His place to dwell in
>> and empower His followers.

He asked that they remain in Jerusalem in prayer.
They did —
> fasting and praying for three days.

At the end of that time,
> they who had hidden themselves behind locked doors
>> now burst into the streets.

In a state of ecstasy, they preached the Christ that so embodied the power and being of the Almighty, that even the chains of death
> and the walls of a tomb could not hold Him.

What got the attention of the pilgrims was the fact that these unlettered men proclaimed the good news in such a dynamic,
> love-filled,

        spirit-filled way,
            that these people heard them speaking in the dialects
                and languages of peoples in countries they knew
                    little or nothing of.
Jews, visiting from all over the world, heard the disciples speak in their own native languages.
Good news, love, and the ecstasy of the soul is like that.
It transcends human languages.

The language barrier, by Hebrew tradition, came about at a place called Shinar, in Babylonia —
    Iraq, if you will,
        thousands of years before this.

With the vehicles of fantasy and humor, the beginning of languages could be told something like this![1]

A long, long time ago, on the plains of Shinar, there lived some people who thought they were special —
    Actually, most of the population of this world lived there.
They had the whole earth to explore and to live in.
That was too easy.
They had their eyes set on bigger game —
    a larger and more mysterious territory —
        heaven itself, where God lives.

These were people who all looked alike,
    talked alike,
        dressed alike,
            thought alike.
One day someone asked what God's house and hunting grounds looked like.
Nobody was too sure.

---

[1] Adapted from a monologue given by Richard Ward of Yale Divinity School, at the Florida Conference (UMC) Institute of Preaching, February, 1993, in Leesburg, Florida. An alternative narrative with a similar monologue is found in Rabbi Marc Gellman's *Does God Have A Big Toe?*, New York, N.Y., 1993.

They assumed it was pretty good —
    all those stars up there —
        and the sun and the moon, and all.
They thought maybe God ought to share it with them.
Someone said, "Let's tell him that."

"Yeah," said another.
"He don't got no right to all that all by hisself.
Who does he think he is, anyway?"

"Suppose he don't like it when we tell him to share?" said another.

Another agitator said, "Who cares?
There's more of us than there is of him.
He gets to run that divine machinery up there that makes the night fall, and the stars come out.
He hurls lightning bolts at us.
I think we could run things better.
We're the best."

Then one of them asked, "Who's gonna tell him?"

They all scratched their heads.
They did that quite often.
That Iraqi desert is full of fleas and lice.
Then one wise guy said, "Never mind that!
How are we going to get to his house?"

"Hmmm," they all said.

"Let's build a tower," someone posed.

"Great idea!" they all exclaimed.
"Uhhh, what's a tower?"
"Let's build a building that gets higher
    and higher

        and higher,
             until it gets up there at his back door.
That's a tower."

"I'm game," they all said.
And so they started building a tower.
Some *made* bricks;
    some *laid* bricks;
        some *carried* bricks.
Day after day, they worked feverishly.
They worked on it for weeks.

Then one day, God had a friend over.
That friend loved God's house,
    especially his back porch,
        where he could look out at all the activity down there on earth.
Ahh, it was beautiful —
    it was a large cabin in the corner of glory land —
        nothing ostentatious, you understand —
            but a great view.
After supper, the friend went out on that porch.
He took a big stretch,
    and looked out at those floating white clouds,
All of a sudden, he noticed a brown speck oozing up through a distant cloud,
    and he yelled, "Hey, God!
        God, come out here!"
It was God's turn to do the dishes.

"Look over there!
What is that?" the friend asked.

"What's what?" asked God.

"Over there in that cloud.
What's that sticking up through the cloud?"

"Just a minute," said God.
"I'll go get my binoculars."

"Why, that's —
　　that's a tower!" God yelled out.

"Well," quipped God's friend, "there goes the neighborhood. What are you going to do?"

God pondered a bit, and said, "I think we'd better go down there."
So they went down,
　　　　down,
　　　　　　down,
　　　　　　　　down,
　　　　　　　　　　from God's back porch to the plains of Shinar.
When they got down there, they stopped a man with a lunch bucket and said,
　　"Excuse me, could you tell us —"

"I'm busy," he snapped.
"I'm going to work on the tower."

They stopped another and said, "Excuse me" —
　　No one would talk with them.

But God was good at solving problems like that, so He said, "Let's follow them."

It wasn't long 'til God's friend said, "Well, there it is."

"There's what?" God asked.

"The tower —
　　the tower," the friend said impatiently.

"They call that a tower?
What a waste of energy."

"What are you going to do?"

"I don't know.
Let me think.
　　Let me think. [*pause — snicker*]
Naaawhh, I couldn't." [*chuckle, chuckle*]

"Couldn't what?
Tell me!
Tell me!"

God pondered some more.
"Nawh, nah."
"Tell me!"

"Have you noticed how they all talk alike?
What would happen if I zapped them and made them speak different languages?" [*snicker*]

　　[*Loud snicker from friend*]

God said, "Well, what do you think?
Are you in?"

"I'm in!
I'm in!"

So the next morning they all came to work.
Some said, "Buenos Dios."
　　Others bowed and said, "Konichiwa."
　　　　Another said, "Guten Tag."
　　　　　"Good morning," said others.
　　　　　　　"Bonjour," said the haughtiest of them all.

"Uhh — give me the hammer," said one.
    And he said it three times.
But it sounded like, "Ughmm — Boba aba uughm uh uh," to the other,
    and he handed him a peanut butter sandwich.

"More mortar and bricks," said someone else, over and over.
    But it sounded more like, "Aagoo pa pama,"
        so he handed him a bucket of oatmeal.
The first thing you know, they had the biggest food fight in history —
    bigger than any you've seen in any of America's junior high schools.

People started running in different directions.
They went to the far corners of the earth,
    just like God intended,
        and they gave up their foolish tower building.
And that's how language began.
Confusion reigned because people,
    unrelated to their Creator,
        became foolish in their pursuits,
            and no longer had in them the heart and soul of their Creator.

They weren't the first, nor were they the last.
And God said, "They need to know me.
We need to be in relationship."
God grieved in His heart and said,
    "It is a people who do err in their heart,
        and they have not known my ways." (Psalm 95:10)

And He came Himself in the body of a man —
    the likeness of a man.
And He came to His very own, and His own received Him not.
It was not the language of their lips that alienated them.
It was the language of the soul.

And He taught,
    He healed,
        He loved,
            yet, they killed Him.
Then He rose from the dead.
And even those of His followers could not quite comprehend.
But, He bade them to pray until their spirits were wedded with His spirit,
    until the language of His soul became their language.
And, they burst forth into the streets with ecstasy,
    communicating across the barriers of human language difference.
And their souls, that resonated with the Creator,
    also resonated with their created brothers and sisters.

Human verbiage is sometimes incapable of expressing the depth of our feelings,
    whether negative or positive.
When we are frustrated,
    enraged,
        fearful,
            we may emit a scream —
                not words —
                      but that scream is full of meaning.
How does one express the depth,
    the breadth,
        the height of his or her feeling when one has found that "special one,"
            that special prince charming, or princess?
How does a mother express her joy when she holds her newborn baby in her arms?
The joy,
    the tenderness,
        and love find no words to express adequately the language of the soul.
But, one who has experienced such love can understand.

Those of you who have experienced the ecstasy of love for God
 can understand how a person can burst forth in human sounds
 that transcend the barriers of language born at Babel.
Now a church is born at Pentecost that surpasses boundaries.
It means that people separated by distance,
 time,
  philosophies,
   and political barriers are united as one.
It means we have a sanctuary for people, whether pro-life or pro-choice,
 whether male or female,
  Greek or Jew,
   smoker or non-smoker,
    liberal or conservative,
     heterosexual or homosexual,
      black or white,
       slave or free,
        Republican or Democrat,
  brilliant or mentally disabled,
   environmentalist or industrialist,
    feminist or feminine.
We have our differences.
Born in confusion and disarray,
 we are united as one soul resonating in response to the love of God.

Babel is no more.
Hallelujah!
Our God reigns!

WE'RE ALL IN THE SAME BOAT
Luke 5:1-11

Chronological studies that try to harmonize the four gospels
depict Jesus as fasting forty days
   and nights in preparation for His ministry.
Immediately after He selected His first disciples:
   Peter,
      Andrew,
         James,
            Philip,
               John,
                  and Nathaniel.
Three days later, He performed His first miracle at a wedding in
Cana —
   the changing of water into wine.
He cleansed the Temple;
   He talked with the Pharisee, Nicodemus, about being "born
   again."
He amazed His disciples by talking with the Samaritan woman at
the well.
His ministry was endorsed by John the Baptist.
At the point of this teaching at Lake Gennesaret,
   it was very early in His ministry —
      perhaps only weeks —
Yet, He was becoming well known,
   attracting large crowds.
He preached to a great multitude at Lake Gennesaret —
   so large and enthusiastic, in fact,
      that the crowd, trying to get close,
         kept backing Him up into the lake.
He stepped into a boat belonging to Simon Peter, James, and
John,
   who were washing and mending their nets at the moment.
When Jesus finished teaching,
   He told the fishermen to launch out into the deep waters for a
   catch of fish.

Simon Peter, the expert fisherman, was a bit impatient with Jesus.
Jesus, after all, knew nothing about fishing.
He was a carpenter and a rabbi.
This was early in his association with Jesus.
Jesus was about to teach him a lesson,
    not just about fishing,
        but about life —
            about Simon's limited perspective —
                about Simon Peter's massive ego,
                    and about who Jesus was —
                        and who Simon was in relation to Jesus.

The Italians have an old folk story they extrapolated from this gospel story to make sense of it from their point of view (The Jesus Tales[2]).
With some modification, it goes like this.

After a long hard day of teaching and healing, Jesus and Peter would go out on the beach.
It was here they talked about problems of the ministry.
It was Peter's job to bring the fish.
It was Jesus' job to bring the wine —
    Jesus had a reputation about that.
This time Peter had more than his share.
He was not a moderate kind of person,
    so, after drinking his fill,
        Peter lay back on the sand,
            looked up at the stars and said,
                "You know, we're doing real good."
The Lord Jesus said, "We?"

Peter says, "All right, all right, all right —
    You're doing real good."
Jesus said, "Me?"

---

[2] Retold by Father John Shea, *Experience An Experience Named Spirit* (Allen, Texas: Thomas More Press), pp. 213-217.

Peter sat up in the sand and looked right across the fire into Jesus' eyes and said,
"All right, All right.
I get it!
God's doing real good."

That made Jesus stand up and dance a jig, right there on the beach.
That dancing got to Peter.
It made him mad.
He said, "You know I wasn't always like this.
Oh, no.
I know how it is now.
People see us and they say, 'There goes the great teacher, Jesus (*hands high*)
    and his sidekick Peter (*hands low*).
        Jesus heals them
            and Peter picks them up.'
It wasn't always like that.
I was the greatest fisherman in all of Galilee."

Jesus said, "Oh, I know you were.
I heard you were a great fisherman!"

"You're darn right I was.
And I'll show you just how good I was.
Let's go fishing.
I'll show you how to catch some fish!"

And the Lord Jesus, who was always anxious to learn about a new career, was very excited.
When they got to the boat, other fishermen looked up.
Their eyes saw something they hadn't seen in a long time.
There was Peter, the great fisherman of Galilee,
    who was in his semi-retirement,
        down there fixing his nets, getting his boat ready,
            and some little guy was with him —

Well —
    they came out in droves;
        some of them got close to the boat;
            and some of them got bold enough to say,
                "Going out today, Peter?"

Peter says, "Yep."

Someone asked, "Mind if we come along?"

Peter says, "Nope."
And he looked up at the Lord Jesus and winked.
Peter was as pompous as an undertaker at a ten thousand dollar funeral.
His ego was so big that when it thundered,
    Peter took a bow.
Well, the Lord Jesus got to ride in Peter's boat.
The Lord Jesus was out front as they went out into the water.
All the boats in the Sea of Galilee followed them.
The Lord Jesus' knuckles were white with fear.
The people thought he was probably afraid of water.

But, Peter was a scientist of a fisherman.
He would lick his finger,
    hold it up in the air,
        and when he felt the wind blowing in a certain direction,
            he would point and growl, "Over there."

The Lord Jesus said, "I'm so excited!"

Peter said, "Shhh!"

All the boats turned and went in the direction the great fisherman had pointed.
When they got to the spot,
    Saint Peter put his finger in the water,
        stirred it and tasted it,
            and said, "They're here!"

The Lord Jesus stood up and yelled excitedly, "Where? Where?
    I don't see any!"

"Shhh," said Peter.

All the fishermen,
    as if on cue,
        began to lower their nets down into the water.
They were looking at each other,
    grinning,
        as if this was going to be the biggest catch they ever had.
Nobody was looking at the Lord Jesus,
    who took a messianic finger —
        tapped it on the bottom of the boat,
            and all the fish in the Sea of Gennesaret dove to the
            bottom.

Saint Peter lifted his arms as if in prayer —
    for he had learned a few things on the road with Jesus —
        and solemnly said, "Raise the nets."

All the fishermen got excited.
They pulled and pulled,
    and their brawny biceps bulged,
        and they pulled and pulled.
The nets surfaced —
    and they were empty.
Somebody in the back started to laugh,
    "Greatest fisherman in all of Galilee, my grandmother's bald
    head.
    He don't know anything.
    We've been out here the best part of the night, and we haven't
    caught a thing.
    Come on!"
And they all began to turn and go back in the direction from
which they came.

When they left, Peter licked his finger and pointed, while Jesus rowed.
So it went all night long.
Peter tasted the waters, and Jesus lowered the nets —
    and the nets came up empty.
Finally, Peter set the sails and came into the land,
    where a crowd was watching,
            working,
                and waiting.
Peter, with a disgruntled growl, joined the other fishermen cleaning their nets,
    while Jesus preached to a crowd that barely let him come ashore.
They crowded to be near him as he taught.
Jesus had to either get in the boat, or drown.
When he finished speaking, Jesus nodded Peter's way and said,
    "Launch out into the deep, and let your nets down for a catch."
This really annoyed Peter, the expert fisherman,
    and he said, with an edge in his voice,
        "Lord, we fished all night, and we caught nothing,
            but if you say, I will let down the net."
The Lord Jesus reached over the side of the boat, and tapped it with his messianic finger.
And all the fish at the bottom began to stir and began to rise to the top —
    at first two by two,
        then ten by ten,
           fifty by fifty,
                and one hundred by one hundred
                    they committed mass silvery suicide,
                        jumping even right into Peter's lap
                            and began slapping him in the face.
When he did let down the net, they caught so many fish that their net was breaking.
They signaled to their partners, James and John, in the other boat, who gave assistance.

There were so many fish that both boats began to sink.
On the shore, all the fishermen began to say,
    "Peter, you old dog you —
        you knew all along where they were."
They hoisted their hero on their shoulders,
    and Peter said, "Put me down!"

Peter began to discover that a man full of himself is likely to be empty,
    and he fell to his knees before Jesus and said,
        "Depart from me, oh Lord, for I am a sinful man."

And Jesus said to Simon, "Do not be afraid.
From now on you shall be fishers of men."
From now on you will have an abundant catch —
    people —
        large numbers of people.

And they left "everything" —
    perhaps even their astonishing catch —
        and followed him on a mission they could not comprehend.
Peter, James, and John responded in awe to the power —
    the power they understood comes from God.
Before this moment, these disciples may have thought themselves as good as they needed to be,
    but along came a revelation which shocked them in its contrast.
They wanted to follow —
    to be a disciple of Jesus Christ.

It is good for us, as well,
    to have a proper perspective of who we are,
        and who our God is —
            to rise up and follow Him.

SECTION III
Concluding Remarks:
Suggestions For Making Monologues

MAKING MONOLOGUES

I. CREATING MONOLOGUES

A monologue generally involves a Biblical character that is familiar to the audience. When one uses a major character as a subject, it usually makes the task easier. When dealing with a major character, the question is not where do I get enough material, but, since I have a limited time span, what do I leave out. The task for that kind of monologue is to keep centered on the elements that illustrate the theme, central idea, or personality characteristics to be developed. Such was the problem with developing the monologue on Peter. I took the occasions that centered on his tendency to open his mouth when he might have done better to keep it shut. With Adam, since it was Mother's Day, I chose to center on his "relationship" with Eve. Given the sheer length of these stories, there were many options I could have taken.

Choosing a major character also has its pitfalls. Some of the old saints have read and heard sermons on the major characters to the point of "anesthetization." To avoid this, one can choose little-known characters; sometimes, in fact, one can discuss a major character from the point of view of a minor character, who is an associate. Accordingly, I chose Reuben to discuss Joseph. There are other advantages to selecting minor characters, such as seeing the event from a viewpoint that is unusual. Additionally, the person in the pew is not likely to be a "great hero." The unheralded play significant roles, but seldom get credit for their deeds. Reuben lived in the shadow of Joseph. How does that feel? A final advantage of choosing a lesser-known character is to enlarge the audience's familiarity with the broader scope of the Biblical narrative.

Sometimes the character is so minor as to be unnamed — almost imaginary. These people can be a useful vehicle to make a point that is otherwise difficult to make. For example, the "Monologue of a Saint" was preached in the season of Pentecost, which I didn't want to ignore. At the same time, it was my first Sunday in a tiny country parish. I wanted the people to know me, as well. This "eyewitness" to Pentecost, dwelling now in God's heaven, was chosen as an all-seeing, all-knowing witness to the ongoing spread of the gospel. She/he even observed God's grace as it was applied to my life, and that of my family. In "Homesick: The Monologue of an Ancient Hebrew," I try to present to the congregation the reasons why an unknown exiled Jew longed for the Temple. He explains the background with a vibrancy that challenges worshipers to think about the anonymous persons who wrote scripture.

One's imagination need not stop there. The perspective does not need to be human. Someday I'm going to create a monologue in which Balaam's ass, who spoke to the prophet, also speaks to this generation. What would the olive tree that lived in the garden where Jesus prayed have to say to us? Many of those olive trees are still there. They "heard" Jesus speak, perhaps they heard the prophets before Him speak, and they've seen history transpire up till the current time. How would an olive tree interpret history in the light of Jesus' prayers? And, do you suppose it might have been an adjacent tree in the garden that was cut down to be the crosses on which three "criminals" hung? The possibilities are endless.

In some cases the Biblical text gives a lengthy story — perhaps too lengthy even to cover in a fifteen to twenty minute monologue sermon. What does the text tell you? Only rarely is it enough just to tell the story. Interpretation is needed. Some of that interpretation is readily available from other Biblical sources. Some of the background information and interpretation may have to be gathered from Biblical commentaries, Bible dictionaries, archaeological reports, and ancient maps. What do these sources tell you about the geography, climate, history, culture, family, system, and persons with which your character interacts?

Such information must then be sifted through an empathic imagination. This is essential to understand the character's inner life and spirit. What sources influenced the character's thinking, behavior and decision making? What would contemporary sociologists, psychologists, and communication theorists have to say that casts light on the behavior of the character? Notice that my monologues often inject contemporary theories to interpret. The character must introduce those theories herself, himself, or itself, however. Perceptual theory can be used to explain how Peter and the disciples could be so blind to the understanding or grasping of Jesus' message. So, Peter, as "Rocky Barjona," helps us to understand him and his fellows by the use of theory and instances in our own culture and day.

Behind every great Biblical story is a much larger and greater one. In order to understand the character, do a task analysis. What individual steps are missing? What took place, for example, in the life of Joseph between the time he was sold into slavery by his brothers, and the next time we encounter him, in Potiphar's house in Egypt? Visualize the scenes traveling to Egypt with the Midianites. What kind of people were they? How might they have treated him in general? Were there any specific personalities that stand out negatively — greedy, grasping, sadistic — or positive people with a fatherly, motherly, brotherly concern? What emotions did Joseph experience? How did he deal with those emotions of betrayal, abandonment, and loneliness? Could he understand their language or dialect? What kinds of visions of his future did he have? What did he pray about? How did he react to the slave market in Egypt? Do we have any parallels in the diaries and writings of pre-Civil War slaves in the United States? How did Joseph react to his new owner? What was it about Joseph that made the new master show a special interest? Could the master have been a "Samaritan" who went out of his way to cultivate the lad? If so, how? What was Potiphar's wife like? Was Joseph the first, or did she, like some slave masters in the United States, commonly exploit some of the young slaves? Why? What did she look like, or act like? Was she a serious temptation for Joseph, or a bitter and repulsive old crone?

When Joseph was in Egypt, how did a foreign tongue and culture affect him? When in prison, were there other Jewish lads? How were they received? How did Joseph feel about doing a "righteous thing," yet finding himself languishing in prison as a result? Where did he think Yaweh was in all this? As a lad, how much did he know about his own God? What was his prison routine? What promises do the scriptures offer that give us insight on such issues as suffering, God's answer to prayers, and so forth? If you, between your knowledge of scripture and your empathetic imagination, can answer the majority of the above questions, you have a basis for a sermon that will reach the hearts of people who already have a special place for Joseph, not to mention those who are just getting acquainted with this special character.

All the above questions assume that there is a distinct viewpoint. Storytelling should let the story make that viewpoint clear. Merely telling events will not suffice. A theme is required. Just as a good research paper, magazine article, or speech has a thesis, or central idea, which sums up the whole in a single sentence, so must a monologue have a central idea statement out of which all scenes, sayings, events, and conflicts grow. It should be stated within the monologue in a variety of ways. Each aspect of the development requires a transition statement that subtly ties the story element back into that main theme.

What is the character saying to the audience? Does that character clearly develop that thought in each situation presented? With some Biblical characters, there is an awesome amount of material. Abraham, Moses, Jesus, Peter, and Paul each are described very fully in a variety of scenes. Each of these scenes may in itself be interesting, even fascinating, but does it readily contribute to the theme the character is developing in this monologue? Would it be better left to another monologue or sermon?

In developing "viewpoint" the monologist must ask not only what is the theme of the monologue, but through whose eyes is it viewed. I tend to think of the monologist as speaking in the first person, as though she/he were the character. Others prefer to tell the story from the third person, as the omniscient observer. There are advantages to each. Telling the story using

"I" is more direct. The audience sees it from inside the character's head. On the other hand, it can be more demanding when one uses the first person. The monologist using first person may require makeup and costuming. She/he must be prepared to be vocally and visually dramatic as the pathos of the story unfolds. It is also argued by those who prefer the third person that one can switch between characters more easily. I disagree. It is just as easy to tell what another person said to you, or apparently thought. One can report what one has heard by rumor. There are many ways to reflect on external events. One does not have to be an omniscient third party. There are advantages to both styles. How one feels comfortable in a given circumstance is the primary consideration. There is one serious limitation, however, to first person monologues. That is the gender limitation. It is most awkward to pretend to be a member of the opposite sex. On one occasion, I tried to be female. I spoke of "running, with my hair flying in the breeze." I almost drew guffaws since I am not only male, but also balding. The use of third person delivery mode would have worked much more advantageously.

Finally, in developing the character, avoid the "B-Movie" syndrome. What is the "B-Movie" syndrome? It is the tendency to make the "good guys" too good — too obvious, and the bad guys too evil and nasty. Life is more complex than that. The more challenging characters are not so simple. In the story of the prodigal son, for example, most of us can identify with all three characters. Indeed, we may end up wondering who is the good guy, and who is the bad guy.

In the monologue "Satan Comes to Church," Satan, who is the very incarnation of evil, is still an attractive, even likable person. Isn't that why we succumb so easily to his "wisdom" and temptations? Isn't this the reason why the apostle Paul says he sometimes comes to us as an angel of light? Characters, like the people we all know, generally have multi-faceted personalities. Chuck Colson (*The Body*, Word Publishing Company, Dallas, pp. 187, 188) tells of the daring kidnapping of Adolf Eichmann by Israeli undercover agents in 1960.

Eichmann was one of the masterminds of the holocaust. Prosecutors called witnesses from the concentration camps. One of the witnesses was Yehiel Dinur. When Dinur entered the courtroom, he stared at Eichmann, now positioned behind bulletproof glass. The eyes of Eichmann (who was responsible for the slaughter of more than a million Jews) met those of Dinur. At first, there was silence, then Dinur began to shout and sob, collapsing to the floor. Why? In a later interview on *60 Minutes*, he explained that it was "because Eichmann was not the demonic personification of evil Dinur had expected. Rather, he was an ordinary man, just like anyone else." Dinur concludes, "Eichmann is in all of us." Thus, one does best to paint personalities as neither overly good nor overly evil. Some of us resolve those conflicts in outrageous ways; others resolve them in a more productive manner — sometimes. Even Jesus was known to get very, very angry. There was a complexity to His human personality as well.

II. ETHICAL PROBLEMS WITH MONOLOGUES

It appears that there are at least two problems with monologues. One of the problems may be unique to monologues; the other is a problem with all sermons — whether and/or how to "borrow" material from others.

The unique problem with monologues is that one is adding extra-biblical material and interpretation blended together with the biblical material, usually without calling attention to which is which. For the biblically literate, they know which is which. Unfortunately, vast numbers of the typical congregation are not going to be familiar with some of the more obscure characters in the Bible. Many won't even be familiar with major characters. The common assumption of the youthful pastor is often that she or he needs merely to interpret the Bible message and stories for the people. We soon learn from blank looks that people don't even know the basic characters, let alone many important themes of the Bible. The monologue is an opportunity to reach the biblically illiterate and the literate, but the biblically illiterate may confuse interpretation with fact. Cautions in the bulletin announcements that one is taking some liberties with the text are in order. A full listing of text citings, with encouragement for the audience to read the text for themselves in the weeks before and after the sermon may help a few. Largely, though, it is a tension one must live with, and/or make clear in the monologue itself — either verbally or non-verbally when the tongue is in the cheek.

With regard to the second issue, borrowing material, credit is best explicitly given upfront. Again, such credit can be given in the bulletin announcement or within the text. No one has any doubt when I borrow extensively, such as I do in sermons in Section II of this book. Many will have heard Walter Wangerin's *Ragman* before, for example.[3] Since that particular monologue is copyrighted, the author and/or publisher will need to be contacted for permission to use it if the material is to be published in any form.

Another problem with borrowing widely circulated material without attribution is that one takes the risk of being regarded as phony, indolent, or by another less than complimentary attribute. The previous pastor may have "borrowed" the same material. A member may have visited another church while on vacation and heard the same sermon. I once welcomed a new family into the community and asked them to come visit our church. The family, as it turned out, was of another denomination and had visited one of its churches in that community the previous week. The man of the house said, with some rancor, that he would visit us, because he had already visited the church of his denomination. It seems that the pastor there read his sermon. Not only had he read it, but it appeared to be the exact same sermon he had heard in another town and another state the Sunday before. More recently, one of our United Methodist District Superintendents here in Florida visited two

---

[3] That particular monologue is copyrighted. The publishers of that material, the material in the appendices, and for scripture quoted from the New Revised Standard Version of the Bible will need to be contacted for permission to use the material if it is to be published in any form.

different Methodist churches under his administration on the same Sunday morning. Two different hours — two different churches, two different communities and two different pastors, yet it was for all appearances the exact same sermon. After checking with them, the superintendent found that they both subscribed to the same sermon service. Though amusing, it probably didn't enhance the credibility of either minister with his superior.

The fact of life is that we all "borrow," consciously or unconsciously, from other sources. No idea, after all, is totally original. There is often a thin line between "borrowing" and plagiarism. One thing that distinguishes is attribution of sources. Another thing that distinguishes the two is that borrowing from one source is more likely to be defined as plagiarism than is borrowing from many sources.

I very clearly "borrowed" from Mark Twain in the monologue "Number One Mother." On the other hand, the vast majority of that monologue is my own material — spawned by reading Twain's *Diary of Adam and Eve*. He tickled my funny bone, and creative energy simply flowed as a result. Had I not attributed my source of some of the material, however, worshipers who have read that story might have said something. Indeed, when I delivered the monologue "Satan Goes to Church," one person did come forward and indicate that some of the material reminded her of C. S. Lewis' *The Screwtape Letters*. Admittedly, there are some slight similarities, but no conscious design, and certainly there are no lines from that work, nor have I read the book in over twenty years.

In the sermon "The End of Babel," I very consciously borrowed from the work of Richard Ward from Yale Divinity. He did a monologue on Babel at a Florida Conference Preaching Institute. I had also read the book by Rabbi Marc Gellman called *Does God Have A Big Toe?* that bears an enormous similarity. It is difficult to know who first wrote what — or even if they both "borrowed" from a similar source — perhaps the Midrashim. However, even with many similarities there are quite significant differences. Gellman's story of Adam also has some similarities with Twain's *Diary*. Again, nothing is "new under the sun." The differences are such in both cases that the works essentially became their own.

III. DELIVERING MONOLOGUES

First person monologues do, as previously indicated, require a sense of the dramatic. Third person does not require quite the same pathos and variety of emotion in the voice. In either case, the monologist will need to be relatively free of notes, spontaneous and lively. That does not mean that the monologue has to be memorized, but the person must appear to be telling a story, not delivering words or reading a manuscript. In general, I believe it best not to memorize monologues or sermons. Sometimes the best creativity occurs at the moment of delivery, just as it would if an individual was telling a story in a conversational setting.

My personal practice after writing a sermon or monologue is to deliver it aloud — usually on a cassette recorder. The process often generates ideas, changes of expression, and some rewriting. I then play the cassette in my car or while brushing my teeth. Sermons, I preach aloud at least three times before entering the pulpit. Monologues that I create, after the rewriting, are transferred to transparencies via the photocopy machine. I preach them while my wife changes transparencies on the overhead projector. While I do not make any serious attempt to follow the wording, the flow is the same. I try to be sure to cue her in by occasionally using some exact wording, particularly as I am coming to the end of a thought written on a given transparency. She then knows to move on. Thus, the material is there if I need it. There is also a transparency feeder machine available through office supply stores that will allow the speaker to change transparencies by a remote switch.

As I write this, our particular sanctuary is built in a semicircle. There are four sections. The machine puts the material on the back wall. I can look at it briefly as I turn to face another section, usually without making it apparent that I am checking my notes. By doing this, I can keep on track and give the illusion of spontaneity, and I don't get hampered with problems that occur with memorization.

I am not particularly making this the recommended way. I am not a person who memorizes well, nor do I like to try to dwell on what I am going to say next. If I were to use the same monologue over and over in different contexts, I am quite sure I would have to find a way to escape using such a "crutch." As a pastor, I do not want my preparation for preaching to be so overwhelming that I am limited in my other pastoral duties. The point is that each of us needs to find a mechanism that gives one substantial freedom from being glued to the pulpit — the freedom to appear, and to somewhat be, spontaneous.

One of the pitfalls of writing out sermons and monologues as I do is the fact that oral style is quite different from written style. Oral style is more likely to be expressed with some incomplete sentences. (See "Herod Speaks" explanatory notes as a sample.) Indeed, we may deliberately use only a word or a phrase instead of a complete sentence, but with a specific tone of voice, the lift of an eyebrow, or a pause that may say far more than a whole paragraph could. The reason I write in "clause format" is to come closer to my oral form. It is also easier for the eye to catch a phrase by itself than read a whole paragraph. The focus almost always needs to be on the thought, not the words. An orientation towards memorizing words will almost certainly destroy the spontaneity of a message. In addition, memorizing has a variety of pitfalls that can be absolutely disastrous.

What is much more important than the words are those nonverbal elements of vocal tone and body language. The nonverbal element is more pregnant with meaning, at least in terms of impact. Albert Mehrabian (*Silent Messages*, Wadsworth Publishing Co., Belmont, California, 1971, 43ff.) states that 93 percent of the impact of a message is nonverbal — 55 percent face and body expression, 38 percent vocal tone. What that means is that no matter how important the words say a gospel principle is, if the minister drones, the nonverbal message emphatically contradicts the verbal. A failure to look at the congregation, a mumbling voice, and a static body strongly suggest the message is not important. This is not to say words are not important. They are. Words give the audience the specifics of the message. Body language and vocal tone give the mood and the thrust of the message. One word can be vocally expressed to convey a much larger message. The word "no!" for example is quite different from "no?" or "nooo."

Delivery of any speech, sermon, or monologue is best when it bears a close resemblance to a conversation. In a conversation, the eyes, hands, body, and voice normally have considerable variety unless we are discussing mathematical tables. When one is conversing about basic values and conflicts, there is a real life in the person who speaks. The Christian minister is discussing things that have cosmic and eternal consequences. This is more than words.

Finally, a word about costumes. If one is a visiting minister and has, therefore, no other responsibility for the worship service or program, complete costumes may be in order. Most of my monologues are delivered as a part of our morning worship. The lectionary provides the theme or character. It is virtually impossible, without a worship leader, to make a complete change of clothing from pulpit robes to the clothing and makeup of a special character. I normally wear a geneva gown and a stole in the pulpit. To change my persona, I need only remove the robe, perhaps to wear an alb (since an alb is not my normal dress), or a thobe (standard white robe mid-easterners wear over street clothing), a yarmulke or just street clothes. I have not always even removed the geneva gown. However, I like to wear something simple to set myself in a different context. To give a visual clue of what I do, I have put pictures with some of the monologues. There are no rigid rules. Every context and congregation may require different modes of dress. Do what works. Be creative in the process.

APPENDIX

A. *Circuit Rider*, a journal for United Methodist clergy in May 1994, p. 7, gives a summary of Michael Williams' suggestions for telling Bible stories. The original also relates to how to use the *Storyteller's Companion*, V. I, p. 23f.

Learning To Tell Bible Stories

- Read the story aloud in at least two translations. You may feel strange reading them aloud, but this will force you to take your time and allow you to notice aspects of the story you never saw before. Pay attention to where and when the story takes place, the characters, objects in the story, and the general order of events.
- Now close your eyes and imagine the story is taking place. You are the playwright/director. Visualize the stage, each act, and each scenery change.
- Look back at the story to make sure you haven't left out any important people, places, things, or events.
- Close all books. Try telling the story aloud to someone (even the family dog will do). Afterwards, ask what questions arise as a result of this telling. Is there information you need about the people, place, things, or language in this story? Is it appropriate to the age, experiences, and interests of those who will be hearing it? Does the story capture your imagination? Remember: you don't have to be able to explain the meaning of a story to tell it.
- Read an exegesis on the story. You may also wish to check a Bible dictionary for place names, characters, professions, objects, or words.
- Once you have the story elements in mind you need to practice, practice, practice. Tell the story ten, twenty-nine, or fifty times over a period of several days. Revise your telling as you go along. Remember, you are not memorizing a text; you are preparing a living event. Each time you tell the story, it will be a little different, because you will be different.

Michael E. Williams, editor
Storyteller's Companion to the Bible

B. The second set of suggestions is found in *Storytelling Magazine* (John Stansfield, "Reclaiming the Past," July 1994, p. 17, used by permission). While it is not a magazine on preaching, nor is the page here cited, this is a magazine that can be of great assistance to the minister who wishes to make dramatic stories, folk-tales, and biographical material a part of his/her other sermons.

Finding the story in history is a challenge that has faced students, parents, and teachers for generations. Here, Colorado storyteller John Stansfield gives insights on how to create, use, and tell stories that bring history to life.

The Creation Of A Historical Tale

Here's how storyteller John Stansfield created a historical tale based on the true achievements of Julia Archibald Holmes.

Use secondary sources
I first encountered information about Julia Archibald Holmes in Gladys Bueler's fine collection, *Colorado's Colorful Characters* (Pruett, 1981). It was less than a page, but this brief reference piqued my curiosity.

Use primary sources
Using Bueler's bibliography, I discovered the curiously titled *A Bloomer Girl on Pikes Peak 1858* (Denver Public Library, 1949) at my local library. It turned out to be a short compendium of Holmes's existing letters and journal entries, along with solid, well-written historical research about her. It was just what I needed to build my story.

Create a subject focus
The heart of the story I chose to develop focuses on the wagon journey the newly-wed Julia made with her husband

and brother on the Santa Fe Trail in 1858, culminating with her ascent of Pikes Peak. Throughout the storyline, I attempted to emphasize issues and concerns most valued by Holmes in her writings. These included: her family and their strongly-held beliefs in abolitionism and women's rights; her burgeoning writing abilities; her sense of wonder in nature and the American West; her determined enthusiasm for life.

Choose a narrative style
I chose a straight-forward, third-person narrative style and interspersed occasional short, yet notable, quotes from Holmes's writings.

Memorize, but don't memorize
Historical stories, for which factuality is important, require more upkeep than other types of stories. Memorizing key facts will help reassure your history-telling, but a story should also flow convincingly through the teller. To foster this atmosphere of trust and understanding, I share Holmes's story in my own and her own words, memorizing only where necessary. This assures that our mutual interest and enthusiasm come through clearly and believably.

Steps To Story Learning
Find an appropriate historical story that you like.
Memorize any verse, direct quotes, dates, statistics, and so forth.
Don't memorize the basic story.
Practice the story in your own words until it becomes tellable.
Tell your story the first time to a sympathetic audience; select a comfortable style and setting.
Consider changing some aspects as you and your story mature. Or find complementary materials for building a thematic program.
Exercise your personal creativity, and keep on telling.

BIBLIOGRAPHY

I. Books

Aristotle, *The Works of Aristotle, V. 8, Britannica, Great Books*, Chicago: University of Chicago, 1952.

Raymond Bailey and James L. Blevins, *Dramatic Monologues: Making The Bible Live*, Nashville: Broadman Press, 1990.

Thomas E. Boomershine, *Story Journey: An Invitation to the Gospel as Storytelling*, Nashville: Abingdon Press, 1988.

Donald Davis, *Telling Your Own Stories*, Little Rock, Arkansas: August House Publishers, 1993.

Mark Galli and Craig Brian Larson, *Preaching That Connects*, Grand Rapids, Michigan: Zondervan Press, 1994.

Marc Gellman, *Does God Have A Big Toe?: Stories About Stories In The Bible*, New York: Harper Trophy, 1989.

Holy Bible: The New International Version, Grand Rapids, Michigan: Zondervan Bible Publishers, 1978.

Holy Bible: The New Revised Standard Version, Iowa Falls, Iowa: World Publishers, 1989.

Holy Bible: The Revised Standard Version, New York: Thomas Nelson, 1952.

Richard A. Jensen, *Thinking In Story: Preaching In A Post-Literate Age*, Lima, Ohio: CSS Publishing Co., Inc., 1993.

Daniel A. Katz and Peter Lovenheim (eds.), *Reading Between the Lines: News Stories From the Bible*, Northvale, New Jersey and London: Jason Aronson, Inc., 1996.

C. S. Lewis, *The Screwtape Letters*, New York: MacMillan Co., 1961.

Romulus Linney, *Jesus Tales: A Novel*, San Francisco: North Point Press, 1980.

Marshall McLuhan, *The Gutenberg Galaxy: The Making of Typographic Man*, Toronto: University of Toronto Press, 1962.

Marshall McLuhan, *The Medium Is The Massage*, New York: Random House, 1967.

Marshall McLuhan and Quentin Fiore, *The Medium Is The Message*, Napa, California: Touchstone, 1989.

Marshall McLuhan, *Understanding Media: The Extensions of Man*, New York: McGraw-Hill, 1964.

Marshall McLuhan and Quentin Fiore, *War and Peace in the Global Village*, Napa, California: Touchstone, 1989.

Albert Mehrabian, *Silent Messages*, Belmont, California: Wadsworth Publishing Co., 1971.

The National Storytelling Festival, *Best Loved Stories at the National Storytelling Festival*, Little Rock, Arkansas: August House Publishers, 1991.

Sydelie Pearl, *Elijah's Tears and Other Stories About the Prophet Elijah*, Cambridge, Masachusetts.: Self-published, 1994.

David P. Polk, *If Only I had Known: Dramatic Monologues*, St. Louis: Chalice Press, 1994.

Lyle Schaller, *The Seven Day A Week Church*, Nashville: Abingdon Press, 1992.

Father John Shea, *Experience An Experience Named Spirit*, (including "The Jesus Tales," retold by Father John Shea, pp. 213-217), Allen, Texas: Thomas More Press.

Mark Twain, edited by Charles Neider, *The Complete Short Stories of Mark Twain* (including the "Diary of Adam and Eve," pp. 272-293), Garden City, New York: Doubleday, 1957.

Walter L. Underwood, *The Contemporary Twelve: The Power of Character in Today's World*, Nashville: Abingdon, 1984.

Walter Wangerin, Jr., *The Book of God: The Bible As A Novel*, Grand Rapids, Michigan: Zondervan Publishing House, 1996.

Walter Wangerin, Jr., *Ragman and Other Cries of Faith*, San Francisco: Harper & Row, 1984.

Richard Ward, *Speaking From The Heart: Preaching With Passion*, Nashville: Abingdon, 1992.

William D. Watley and Susan D. Johnson Cook, *Preaching in Two Voices: Sermons on the Women in Jesus' Life*, Valley Forge, Pennsylvania: Judson Press, 1992.

Elie Wiesel, *Sages and Dreamers: Biblical, Talmudic, and Hasidic Portraits and Legends*, New York: Summit Books, 1991.

Michael E. Williams, editor, *The Storyteller's Companion to the Bible*, Nashville: Abingdon Press, 1991 ff. Currently vols. 1-9 are in print.

Interpreter's Dictionary of the Bible, 4 volumes, Nashville: Abingdon Press, 1962.

II. Periodicals

Anna Carter Florence, "The Inheritance," *Pulpit Digest* LXXV (November/December, 1994), pp. 5-10.

John Stansfield, "Reclaiming the Past: Storytelling and Education," *Storytelling* 6 (July, 1994), pp. 16, 17.

John Sumwalt, "The Healing Power of Stories," *Circuit Rider* 18 (May, 1994), pp. 4-7.

Martin Theilen, "Beyond Infosermons," *Leadership* XV (Winter, 1994), pp. 38-43.

Tom Younger, "Why I Use Other People's Stuff," *Leadership* XV (Winter, 1994), pp. 66, 67.

Weavings: A Journal Of The Christian Life (Theme is "Remember the Story") IV (January/February, 1989).

"News & Trends: Lessons For A Stuck Society," *Psychology Today* vol. 25 (September, 1992), p. 8.

East Tennessee State University's Storytelling Master Degree Program, *Storytelling World*. ETSU, Box 70647, Johnson City, Tennessee 37614-0647. Issued quarterly.

The Journal of the Network of Biblical Storytellers, *The Journal of Biblical Storytelling*. Dayton, Ohio. Published occasionally.

III. Video Tapes

    Doug Lipman, *Coaching Storytellers: A Demonstration Workshop For All Who Use Oral Communication*. Jonesborough, Tennessee: National Storytelling Association, 81-minute VHS.

IV. Audio Tapes

    Richard Ward, "Institute of Preaching," February 21-23, 1994, 3 tapes, Florida Conference of the United Methodist Church. Purchase from Don Heishman, 4444 US 98 N. #388, Lakeland, Florida 33809.

    "Storytelling — Like Loaves and Fishes," *Conference on Storytelling and Preaching*, June 18-23, 1995, Kanuga Conference Center, Hendersonville, North Carolina 28793.

V. Professional Associations

    The Network of Biblical Storytellers
    1810 Harvard Blvd.
    Dayton, Ohio 45406
    1-800-355-NOBS

    This is a group that believes that *biblical stories* have "the power to transform individual and communal lives." Membership is $30.00 per year. They publish a quarterly journal and schedule conferences to train and encourage people in the art of telling biblical stories.

    The National Storytelling Association
    P. O. Box 309
    Jonesborough, Tennessee 37659

    The National Storytelling Association sponsors festivals and is publisher of *Storytelling Magazine*. In addition, most states have a chapter. Addresses can be obtained through the National Association.